You could be Dancing

The discovery of a life, love, hope and happiness that leads you home.

REBECCA MOORE

 A catalogue record for this book is available from the National Library of Australia

You Could Be Dancing
Copyright © 2023 Rebecca Moore

Published by Star Label Publishing
P.O. Box 1511, Buderim, QLD, Australia
publishing@starlabel.com.au

All rights reserved. No part of this publication may be reproduced in any form; stored in a retrieval system; or transmitted; or used in any other form; or by any other means without prior written permission of the publisher (except for brief quotes for the purpose of review or promotion).

All Scripture quotations unless otherwise indicated are from The Holy Bible, New International Version®, NIV® Copyright © 1973, 1978, 1984, 2011 by Biblica, Inc.™ Used by permission. All rights reserved worldwide.

Scripture quotations marked (ESV) are from The Holy Bible, English Standard Version® (ESV®), copyright © 2001 by Crossway, a publishing ministry of Good News Publishers. Used by permission. All rights reserved.

Scripture quotations marked (MSG) are taken from The Message. Copyright © 1993, 1994, 1995, 1996, 2000, 2001, 2002. Used by permission of NavPress Publishing Group.

The views expressed here-in remain the sole responsibility of the author, who exempts the publisher from all liability. The author and publisher do not assume responsibility for any loss, damage, or disruption caused by the contents, errors or omissions, whether such contents, errors, or omissions result from opinion, negligence, accident, or any other cause, and hereby disclaim any and all liability to any party.

ISBN: 978-0-6484602-1-3

Bono and Raphi.

CONTENTS

ACKNOWLEDGEMENTS	vii
INTRODUCTION	ix
1. Why hello there …	3
2. Sometimes love hurts	7
3. Second chances	11
4. We live in a beautiful world	15
5. Put some salt on it	19
6. Take it to the top	23
7. And on earth, peace	27
8. The topsy turvy world of God	31
9. Warnings	35
10. Poem – little bird	41
11. The Island that prays together, stays together	45
12. The thing about that goat	49
13. Shine bright like a diamond	55
14. Stop! It's coffee time	59
15. So ... what hope do we have?	63
16. Guess how much i love you?	69
17. Life, parenting and yapping ankle-biters	73
18. Three ways to help your children cope with fear	77
19. Dressed for success	83
20. Poem – Little Boat called Hope	89
21. Words for dinner	93

22. List makers, relax!	97
23. Every thread counts	101
24. No time for accusations	105
25. Are we there yet?	109
26. One, two, three … look at me	117
27. Peace on earth	121
28. Thank you Jesus! A word for those that worry	125
29. The cheerful giver	129
30. Poem – She dances	135
31. Downton Abbey and a trip through another age	137
32. Words of comfort	141
33. The Little Boat called Hope	145
34. Christmas, gatherings and eternal treasures	149
35. Let your light shine	153
36. He lifted up our car!	157
37. Catch my fall	161
38. The night of the lasagna disaster	165
39. Have I loved you enough today?	169
40. Poem – It's you	175
ABOUT THE AUTHOR	179
ALSO BY REBECCA MOORE	181

Previously titled First To Forty...

This book was previously titled *First to Forty* and was published as a special gift from my husband for my fortieth birthday. The title *First to Forty* referred to the first 39 of my first published articles and poems, with the fortieth being a poem written by my husband.

However, the title proved more confusing than intended and so, has led to its rebirth under the new title,
You Could Be Dancing.

My intention for this book is to share the words that have come from my walk with Jesus through some difficult times, with the realisation that even though trials and adversity come your way, if you hold onto the promises of God, you will triumph, and you could be dancing.

I hope that these words will bless and encourage you to find your way closer to Jesus everyday as we make our way home.
I hope you enjoy it.

ACKNOWLEDGEMENTS

To my ever-loving husband, who painstakingly went to the trouble to have my first forty published articles put into book form, surprising me with it for my fortieth birthday. How blessed I am to walk through this life with you by my side.

To my children who inspire so much of what I write – the world is a more beautiful place because you are here.

To our parents who trained us in the way we should go – it is a very good way indeed.

To all those who supported me in my early writing endeavours – thank you.

And to God, my Heavenly Father.
Jesus, You are my home, my rest, my salvation.
Your Spirit dwells within.

INTRODUCTION

You Could be Dancing is written from a heart searching and finding God in the midst of everyday life, and choosing God's perspective over the world's. Though life is full of trials and tribulations, there is a space where God dwells within us, where His 'peace that passes all understanding' exists. When the world may seem crashing about us, the sweet small voice of God can be heard if we are still and listen. The more we listen, the more recognisable His voice becomes, until it becomes the main voice that we hear.

You Could be Dancing invites you to let go of that which weighs you down and to feel the lightness of the freedom which comes from above. It takes you on a journey through the everyday-ness of life, the ordinary and not-so-ordinary, the trials and triumphs, to hear His voice and find our way back home to the safety, love, and peace of Jesus.

Chapter 1

WHY HELLO THERE....

Why hello there. So nice to see you. You look exhausted, come sit with me a while. Take off your shoes, wipe the sweat from your brow.

I see you're still pushing your wheelbarrow around. Your load has grown since last I saw you. It must be heavy. No wonder you feel tired.

Let's see what you have in there. Oh yes, you still have hurts from two years ago and that nasty thing your cousin said when you were five. You've kept the apple that was thrown at you at school. The hurtful glare from your neighbour is polished and well preserved. Looks like you have cared for these things with great attention. Not one detail is missing.

How full are the other wheelbarrows?

You know, the ones of your friends and acquaintances. Have you deposited into them lately? Yes, I did say deposited.

No? So, you've never offended anyone? Think carefully, I'm sure there must be something.

You didn't think about that did you? They must be tired too. Tired of pushing around old hurts from the past.

Let's try taking some things out of your wheelbarrow. That's it. Pick one up and have a good look at it. Is holding on to that going to add anything to your life? Just place it over here.

Now, try lifting the wheelbarrow again. It's lighter, isn't it? Yes, it should be easier to push now. Go on and give it a try. Haha! That's great. Spin it around and run it up that hill.

Now, now, don't look longingly at what's been removed. It only weighs you down. I know you've become used to it. It's almost been a comfort to you, a companion. It justifies your actions, excuses your moods. It gives you reason to withhold from or punish others.

Time to let go of your wheelbarrow
It's time to let go of your wheelbarrow. I know someone you can leave it with. He will take good care of it for you. That's it, now go and tell your friends.

Yes, I can see! You are running, now skipping and yes ... even dancing. It's so much easier without your wheelbarrow.

Don't forget to tell your friends. They will love the feeling of releasing it too.

Remember, you can't get close to people if there's always a wheelbarrow coming between you.

> Come to me, all you who are weary and burdened, and I will give you rest. Take my yoke upon you and learn from me, for I am gentle and humble in heart, and you will find rest for your souls. For my yoke is easy and my burden is light.
> (Matthew chapter 11 verses 28-30)

Chapter 2

SOMETIMES LOVE HURTS

When my children were babies, I tended to their every need. I nursed them, held them and sang over them. I let them know at every opportunity that they were loved, secure and safe.

As they grew, my love took on new forms. I still loved on them with hugs and comfort, but my role became more active as I watched every move of my adventurous toddlers.

To keep them safe would sometimes require discipline. A strict scolding could warn them to get off the road where they could be hurt or worse. Throwing myself in the face of danger that my little ones couldn't see was part of my protective mothering role and one that couldn't be taken lightly.

These precious little children were a gift to me from God and it was my job to look after them to the best of my ability.

Regardless of how tired I was or if I had something else I wanted to do at the time, none of that mattered as much as keeping them safe, sound and secure.

As they grew, they learned to do more for themselves under my watchful eye. Letting them spread their wings was also a beautiful process of recognising where their talents lay and watching their skills develop in areas I am still so amazed to see.

But throughout all of this growth, the good is mixed with a whole lot of struggles. Discipline is never fun and for a child, it is hard to see the reasoning behind it:

"Why can't I put the basting brush in the microwave and turn it on until it catches fire?"

"Why shouldn't I climb the fence when I am two years old and run through the neighbour's yard?"

"Why shouldn't I go down the steep driveway headfirst on my skateboard at three years old with my glasses on?"

"Why shouldn't I jump on the bonnet of Daddy's favourite car? It's just like a trampoline!"

As my children grew older, they learned to trust me a little bit more. I think they worked out that maybe mum knows a thing or two.

As an adult

As an adult, I look at the times God has had to discipline me. It's never comfortable and it can be downright painful. At times I have not understood it at all, and sometimes I even thought God was being mean.

But when I reached the other side of the trials, the words that came from my mouth were: "I'm glad I went through that – but I would never want to go through that again!"

Hopefully those lessons have been learnt, and there are sure to be new ones. When I reflect, I see myself wrestling in the discomfort of the situation, just as my toddlers would wrestle in being stuck in a pram or a car seat. I wrestled until I surrendered. With my hands in the air, I came to a place where I would say, "Not my will but yours God".

That's when the peace would come. Even though the situation may not have changed, what had changed was me and the realisation that maybe my Father in Heaven knew what was good for me better than I did.

Trying to control the future is not even on my list now. Who can know the mind of God? I do know, however, that He has my best interests at heart and that, just as I love my children and can generally see what is good and what is bad for them, God loves us so much more and can clearly see what is up ahead.

He is the deliverer of our daily bread, knowing what we need for each moment and knowing what we are to become through our trials and our pain. God has a knack of creating beauty out of ashes. It is a matter of surrender. It is a matter of trust.

> ... I will refine them like silver and test them like gold. They will call on my name and I will answer them; I will say, 'They are my people,' and they will say, 'The Lord is our God.'
>
> (Zechariah chapter 13 verse 10)

Chapter 3

SECOND CHANCES

Arriving to interview a lady for a story a while back, I was feeling prepared. My voice recorder was charged and ready, I had my list of questions ready to go and I was early.

As I stepped out of my car, my glass water bottle fell to the ground and started rolling down the street. As I ran to retrieve it, I dropped my phone, my shoe strap came undone, and I was pretty sure I looked anything but prepared.

I quickly picked up my phone, checking that the screen was still in one piece, and scurried to retrieve my water bottle from the gutter a few metres away. I grinned to myself as I sat back in my car. I must have looked fairly ridiculous at this point, but hey, sometimes you just have to laugh at yourself.

Pulling myself together and fixing my rogue shoe strap, I checked my phone. *Running late, be there soon – Dawn.*

"Oh, thank goodness!" I thought. She was running late and didn't even see my circus performance. As waves of relief washed over me, I prepared for entrance number two, which, may I say, was much more graceful and ladylike, and I was grateful for a second chance.

Second chances
As I sat and listened to Dawn's inspiring story of how her life had changed from being a rollercoaster of financial and business success, to a life of serving others after a tragic bout of illness, I began thinking about second chances.

Teaching teenagers about self-worth and providing workshops for women who had survived and escaped from domestic violence was a far cry from the insecure, hurt young girl that she had once been. But once God showed up in her life, she was never the same.

Transformations
When I think about miracles, it's not always the instant healings that come to mind. It is the transformation of lives.

I don't know if there is such a thing as a clean-cut Christian. To need a saviour means that we have needed to be saved from something. To have God send His son to die for our sins means that we were so far gone, there was no way we could save ourselves. No amount of rituals, sacrifice or religiosity was going to help us. We needed a God who loved us and the only one possible, was the Creator Himself.

It's phenomenal
And that's where we get to see His glory. Not just in the phenomenal existence of millions of galaxies; not just the amazing way the sun creates a different portrait in the sky for each sunset; not just by the incredible gift of new life every time a baby is born and that not one fingerprint is the same – but His glory is also seen in the transformation of lives; of God taking something that seems worthless, deserted and of no worth in the eyes of others, and putting worth back into it; breathing new life into it; holding it in His hands and gazing at it with so much pride and love, knowing that it is very good – and that this was worth dying for.

Even in our mess
When God finds us in our mess of life, He is not repelled. He is waiting for us to reach our weary, tired hand in the air and say, "Help!" Nothing will hold Him back. He will race to you with a swoosh and an all-encompassing bounty of love. In fact, all of heaven will rejoice. He's just waiting to love us and repair us and welcome us back into His fold.

Luke chapter 15 verses 1 to 7 tells us of the man who left his 99 sheep to find the one that wandered off.

And when he finds it, he joyfully puts it on his shoulders and goes home. Then he calls his friends and neighbours together and says, 'Rejoice with me: I have found my lost sheep.' I tell you that in the same way there will be more rejoicing in heaven over one sinner who repents than over ninety-nine righteous persons who do not need to repent.

Go on, put your hand up.

Chapter 4

WE LIVE IN A BEAUTIFUL WORLD

Don't laugh now, but the thought of snorkelling has always made me a little nervous. Breathing through a pipe while having your nose blocked made the word 'claustrophobic' come to mind, so I never felt the need to go out of my way to try it. That was, of course, until we visited Queensland's Great Barrier Reef.

"You can't go to the Barrier Reef and not go snorkelling!" I was told. So, I decided to *woman-up* and give it a go, and I am so glad I did.

A whole new world
After calming my initial panic-breathing into long deep relaxing breaths, I was welcomed into a world I had never before experienced outside of photos. This underwater world was beautiful. The coral, in so many colours and forms, some swaying to the rhythm of the water, was home to extraordinary sea life and reef fish.

As the sun shone down giving life to this secret underwater world, it exposed a kaleidoscope of colours of iridescent purples, yellows, blues and greens emanating from the coral and the fish – each creature so uniquely different and so uniquely beautiful working together as a perfect underwater community.

Under threat
According to greatbarrierreef.com, one of the greatest threats to the protection of the reef is also one of its greatest strengths:

> *... the level of utter dependence each part of the ecosystem has on one another. That is to say, that if a single organism or species is affected or declines in number, it can have a huge ripple effect both down and up through the Great Barrier Reef's food chain.*

Shipping accidents, oil spills and overfishing amongst other things, greatly affect the health and ongoing care of the reef. Processes have been put in place to help protect this underwater playground and as tourists, we were instructed on how to respectfully treat this beautiful heritage listed area.

Beauty in people

When I look around me in the human world that we live in, I see such beauty here too. I know people who are extraordinary artists who colour the world with their visual imagery. I see dancers who move me to tears. I know people who are always looking to help the lonely or needy, changing lives by the fact that they think beyond themselves.

I know people who play amazing music which speaks to the soul in ways words cannot; people who create beautiful garments out of a roll of material; people who serve their lives to give health to others through the medical profession. People who risk their lives to save others from dangerous situations; those who find joy in educating the next generation whether it be through school, music, art, or sport – this is their passion.

Pollution

I look at these things and I notice how quickly the beauty of people can be pushed aside by the distraction and pollution of devastating news reports of the evil and atrocities that daily affect our world and the people who live in it.

I see, just like the reef, when one part of our world hurts, it affects the rest of it, sometimes with huge ripple effects. But there is still so much beauty to be seen in each one of us and good must triumph over evil.

Working together

If we take the gifts that have been given to us, and allow the Son to shine through them, balance can be added to this unbalanced world, hope to hopelessness, joy to misery and colour to grey dark days.

1 Corinthians tells us that as the church, we have been put together each with our own gifts to make up one body of many parts. And the body needs all parts.

> ... in fact God has placed the parts in the body, every one of them, just as he wanted them to be. (chapter 12 verse18)

Your part is important so don't underestimate what God has given you. The Bible tells us He made you and formed you in your mother's womb. He is purposeful in what He makes, and He has a purpose for you. You have a purpose in the great scheme of things and whether it be noticed or not, the body needs you. Help make this world beautiful and let your light shine.

> For we were all baptised by one Spirit so as to form one body – whether Jews or Gentiles, slave or free – and we were all given the one Spirit to drink. Even so the body is not made up of one part but of many.
> (1 Corinthians chapter 12 verses 13-14)

Chapter 5

PUT SOME SALT ON IT

My family enjoys nice tasting food. Despite a few standout failures, I can usually deliver on this, but recently we ran out of one small ingredient – salt.

I had almost bought a new packet of salt at the supermarket but was sure I had a refill at home, so I left it. That night as dinner was being served, I searched the cupboard for the refill pack but to no avail. There was no salt and our side dish of poached eggs tasted rather bland.

More than just flavour
There are some foods like hot chips that just seem to scream for the flavour of salt. Salt can even enhance sweet food like salted caramel for example.

It is good for other things too. Salt is a: preservative; flavour enhancer; colour enhancer; texture enhancer; nutrient source; and a binder. Basically, it is vital to our survival.

Healing in the water

As I opened my Bible to 2 Kings the next morning, I was amused to find that the first passage I laid my eyes on was about salt. What was God trying to tell me?

The scene was set during the time of the prophet Elisha. To give you the basic idea, the people of the city were baffled.

Their town was well situated with everything as it should be, but the water was bad, and the land was unproductive for no apparent reason.

The people of the town approached Elisha regarding this problem. Their crops were suffering, and they couldn't understand why.

In response, Elisha said, *"bring me a new bowl."* He told them to put some salt in it, then he went to the spring and threw the salt into the water saying:

> This is what the Lord says: 'I have healed this water. Never again will it cause death or make the land unproductive.'

As promised, the water was cleansed and the land became productive again and has remained pure to this day according to the word Elisha had spoken, (paraphrased from 2 Kings chapter 2 verses 19-22).

Salt of life

When I think about different areas of my life, there are those that stand out as flourishing and others that could use a little help, or a little 'salt'. The preparation has been done, the 'soil' is good, the circumstances around them are all as they should be, all that's needed now is for God to come and touch it and make it salty, bringing flavour, health and life to it.

You may, right now, be thinking of areas in your life that feel stunted, lacking life and vitality. Maybe those areas need some salt shaken on them in the form of prayer.

By making an effort to pray for God's help in these areas, He can add flavour and prevent decay, enhance the sweetness, colour and life so that when the time comes for these areas to flourish, they will be full of vitality and health straight from the hand of God.

Be the salt-seasoning

It is not just the 'areas' in our lives that need salt, salt begins with who we are in Christ. Just as a kind word or a smile from someone lifts your spirit and gives you joy, when we are full of God's saltiness, we can't help but affect others with it.

You'll be glad to know, buying salt was high on my agenda the following day and our food once again had a full-bodied flavour that made everyone happy. If that food loses its saltiness, well – it just won't be worth eating now, will it?

Let me tell you why you are here. You're here to be salt-seasoning that brings out the God-flavours of this earth. If you lose your saltiness, how will people taste godliness?

(Matthew chapter 5 verse 13 MSG)

Chapter 6

TAKE IT TO THE TOP

Climbing Mt Coolum (Sunshine Coast Australia) earlier in the year was a great idea – until we got half way up the slope to the steep incline, which is when our post-Christmas bodies decided maybe this wasn't such a good idea after all. Nevertheless, we pushed forward.

Now to those of you who are pretty fit, you may be laughing right now knowing that Mt Coolum really isn't a difficult climb – and you're right (even I am laughing). Which is why we did our best to look like we were totally enjoying every step as we gave way to the other climbers on the path – not so much out of politeness but rather as an excuse to catch our breath.

My 11-year-old kindly offered to catch up with us on our way back down and his older sister was more than happy to wait and 'look after him' until we got back .

"You're so close to the top, you must keep going!" we encouraged (while secretly enjoying the excuse to stop too).

Breathtaking
You'll be glad to know, we all made it to the top and were rewarded with the breathtaking view of the surrounding mountains and ocean. Even though we were expecting this reward, the thrill of arriving at the top was more wonderful than we first thought.

If we had decided to stop halfway, we would never have known the full extent of what lay ahead for us, and the effort we had already afforded to the climb would have been wasted.

We would have missed this opportunity to soak in the beauty of the expanded horizon exposing lush mountains and stretching ocean as far as the eye could see.

We would have also missed the opportunity to see another part of God's beautiful handiwork from this particular spot, on this particular mountain, on this particular day and remember once again how blessed we are to live in such a beautiful part of the world.

It was worth the struggle.

Worth the struggle
When I read in the Bible stories of people like Noah, Abraham, Moses, and Joshua, to name just a few, I am in awe of how they caught the vision of the dream God had given them and faithfully continued on their paths

even though they were mocked, fought against and pushed back and even though the reward was seemingly humanly impossible and incomprehensible.

Noah was saved from the flood that wiped out the entire world. Abraham received in his old age, the child that was promised him in his younger years. Moses led his people out of slavery and Joshua led them into the promised land.

Along the way, these people saw things that only God could do. Noah may have been ridiculed for building an ark, but it was the only thing that floated when the flood came.

Abraham was told he would be the father of nations even though his wife was barren until she was beyond child-bearing years.

Moses saw the sea part and food fall out of heaven as he led his people to safety.

Joshua saw the walls of the city collapse after leading his army around them for seven days.

Not one of these journeys were easy. Fraught with pain, trials and grief, the strongest man's endurance would have been tested beyond measure.

The impossible is possible
Yet these men knew how big their God was. They knew beyond doubt that He was capable of doing the impossible – and He did. God was and is still faithful.

Whether or not our situations turn out the way we hope and when we hope, believing that God is capable of doing the impossible, makes all things possible. It just requires our obedience and knowledge of the One who is capable of all things.

> You were shown these things so that you might know that the Lord is God: besides him there is no other.
> (Deuteronomy chapter 4 verse 35)

Chapter 7

AND ON EARTH, PEACE

Standing at the service desk of a retail outlet during the Christmas season, I was struck at how constantly the phone was ringing and how frazzled the attendant was, trying to keep up with each demand.

"Gee, you're busy!" I said to the attendant when there was a break.

"Yeah, it's been crazy this morning," she replied. She then continued with, "You know, this time of year is meant to be filled with joy and good tidings, but people have been horrible. I have just been abused over the phone repeatedly in the last five minutes. But I guess people are stressed trying to get everything done."

"Well, I hope you have a happy Christmas," I replied, and with that she smiled and wished the same back to me.

The silly season
Some people call this time of year 'the silly season', the time that marks the end of all activities, culminating their concluding celebrations, concerts, and ceremonies into two small weeks preceding the end of school.

These are beautiful celebrations and to be enjoyed but add to that the rush before Christmas to find 'just the right gift' to give the ones we love while people are pushing in lines, cutting in on carparks, and abusing salesclerks over the phone when their answers aren't quick enough – you can see how things can become a little out of the ordinary.

Let's bring it back a notch
When Jesus first came into the world in simplicity, as a baby wrapped in swaddling cloths and laying in a manger, He was introduced to the shepherds by a great company of angels saying,

> Glory to God in the highest heaven, and on earth peace to those on whom his favour rests.
> (Luke chapter 2, verses 13–14)

When Jesus was comforting His disciples before His crucifixion, He left these words with them:

> Peace I leave with you; my peace I give you. I do not give to you as the world gives. Do not let your hearts be troubled and do not be afraid.
> (John chapter 14, verse 27)

Transcending all understanding
In the hustle and bustle of a noisy world, peace is not in what's going on around you, peace begins in your heart.

Philippians chapter 4, verse 7 tell us that:

> ... the peace of God, which transcends all understanding, will guard your hearts and your minds in Christ Jesus.

It is a peace that remains even:

> ... though the earth give way and the mountains fall into the heart of the sea, though its waters roar and foam and the mountains quake with their surging.
> (Psalm chapter 46, verses 2–3)

I have heard stories of people singing praises to God even when facing death, people going through the worst times in their lives feeling a peace they cannot explain. I have felt it myself in my own insignificant circumstances and it is nothing short of miraculous.

How then, do we find this peace?
We trust in Jesus. We trust that no matter what we've done, what we're going through, He's got our back, He knows more about our situation than we could ever imagine.

He doesn't promise us an easy ride, but He does promise us that, whatever we go through, He will never leave us or forsake us. And we have the added bonus of feeling His presence with us, for nothing can separate us from His love. This, to me, is peace on earth.

Whether they be the frazzled store attendant or the cranky shopper, we too can announce Jesus by carrying a message of peace, just as the angels did on that holy night over 2000 years ago.

> "Though the mountains be shaken and the hills be removed, yet my unfailing love for you will not be shaken nor my covenant of peace be removed," says the Lord, who has compassion on you.
>
> (Isaiah chapter 54, verse 10)

Chapter 8

THE TOPSY TURVY WORLD OF GOD

What if up was down, black was white, left was right and out was in? Sounds a little like the world we live in, don't you think?

It seems that with every passing trend there is a new one to follow. What once was unthinkable is then accepted and then not accepted, and the cycle continues.

For instance, if anyone had told me when I was a child, that in the 90s it would be fashionable for guys to wear their pants halfway down their posteriors with their underwear showing, I would have laughed myself silly.

No offence to those who think that is cool, and I'm sure you are very cool, but back then (and to an eight-year-old girl), that just would have seemed very funny and maybe a little embarrassing.

There were plenty of fashions in the 80s and 90s that were cool at the time, some have even done the full circle and made it back to acceptable, current, and even iconic.

I like the changing of seasons as much as the next person, but I am glad that some things remain unchanged even though they still seem, after many centuries, a little topsy turvy.

In a world where riches and power are highly sought after at any cost, where women and children are being abused and mistreated, where the value of an animal is worth more than an unborn child, and the worship of God is punishable by death, it's reassuring to know that God has never changed and has His own way of keeping things interesting.

The way of the world teaches that advancement is dominance, and to push everyone and everything out of the way in order to promote and advance oneself at the cost of all others is success.

A servant king
Jesus demonstrated the opposite – coming to earth as a servant.

To begin with, He left the glory of His place in heaven to be born in a manger surrounded by animals. He served His disciples by washing their feet. He healed the sick and spent time with the outcasts of society. He showed love to the unlovely and friendship to the lonely and lost.

When questioned about why He ate with sinners, Jesus replied:

> It is not the healthy who need a doctor, but the sick. I have not come to call the righteous, but sinners.
>
> (Mark chapter 2, verse 17)

When two of His disciples requested places of honour in heaven, He told them:

> Whoever wants to become great among you must be your servant, and whoever wants to be first must be slave of all. For even the Son of Man did not come to be served, but to serve, and to give his life as a ransom for many.
>
> (Mark chapter 10, verses 43–44)

Psalm 68 tells how God is a father to the fatherless, a defender of widows setting the lonely in families and leading out prisoners with singing. He displaced kings and armies and allowed the women to come in and collect the plunder, calling the women who proclaim God's word *'a mighty throng'*.

A topsy turvy world
I wonder what it would be like, a world where this behaviour was dominant? Where we lived to serve, rather than be served. Where we lived to give, rather

than receive. Where we lived to promote, rather than be promoted.

A little topsy turvy perhaps? I think it would be unrecognisable and probably not completely possible in this lifetime, but something to think about, nonetheless.

God's topsy turvy world:

> Blessed are the poor in spirit, for theirs is the kingdom of heaven.
> Blessed are those who mourn, for they will be comforted.
> Blessed are the meek, for they will inherit the earth.
> Blessed are those who hunger and thirst for righteousness, for they will be filled.
> Blessed are the merciful, for they will be shown mercy.
> Blessed are the pure in heart, for they will see God.
> Blessed are the peacemakers, for they will be called children of God.
> Blessed are those who are persecuted because of righteousness, for theirs is the kingdom of heaven.
> (Matthew chapter 5, verses 3–10)

Chapter 9

WARNINGS: EVERYONE RECEIVES THEM - THE WISE HEED THEM

The words "bombs away!" stand as a warning that if you are anywhere near or in a pool, you are about to receive the effects of an almighty splash from the clown who thought it would be a good idea to bomb dive into the midst of everyone.

Unfortunately, there is no time to run, as the words are generally shouted at the time of leaping. The best you can do at this point is to duck for cover.

I always find it humorous to be in a shopping centre when an alarm is sounded. It seems that, while a few of us are checking to see if the alarm is a drill or not, the rest of the shopping community continue what they are doing as if nothing is happening.

We are so used to 'drills' that I wonder if we'd be able to save ourselves in the event of a real emergency?

Are you ready?
The Bible is full of warnings, the most exciting is that one day Jesus will be coming back.

The Bible tells us that there will be signs leading up to Jesus' return. In Luke chapter 12 verse 54 Jesus tells us that, just as we know by looking at the clouds if it will rain, so we must look for the signs and be ready for the return of the King.

We could laugh it off and say, "It's never going to happen in my lifetime!" But what if it does? It's got to happen sometime so if it does happen in your lifetime, are you ready?

Exciting times
My nephew is getting married next month. As our family prepares gifts, wedding attire and preparations, we look forward to it with great anticipation. It will be a fantastic celebration filled with joy and we will celebrate with food and dancing.

Just as our family is excited in these preparations, how much more then, should we be excited about Jesus' promised return?

In Matthew chapter 25, verses 1-13, Jesus tells a parable of the ten bridesmaids waiting with their lamps for the groom to arrive. The groom is late, and the oil has run out in the lamps. The five bridesmaids who were prepared brought extra oil and were welcomed into the wedding banquet. Unfortunately, the unprepared bridesmaids were left out.

Don't miss out
Jesus doesn't want anyone to be left out. He wants us to be aware and alert, which is why He has told us about His coming in many different ways, centuries in advance.

There is a whole book in the Bible on the subject of His return called Revelation, not to mention all the prophecies throughout the Old and New Testaments. He has been preparing this for a long time and is so excited for the day when He welcomes us home.

> Do not let your hearts be troubled. You believe in God; believe also in me. My Father's house has many rooms; if that were not so, would I have told you that I am going there to prepare a place for you? And if I go and prepare a place for you, I will come back and take you to be with me that you also may be where I am. You know the way to the place where I am going.
> (John chapter 14 verses 1-4)

The way
And the way is this: God gave His son Jesus to die and take the punishment for all our sins. You see, He wants us with Him so much, He made it as easy as possible for us, even though it cost Him more than we can imagine, yet we allow so many distractions to cloud out the simple truth.

God won't force you to believe because He gave you the gift of free will, but He gives us chances. He's already done the hard work and the rewards are incredible and eternal.

He is longing to welcome you home.

> He will wipe every tear from their eyes. There will be no more death or mourning or crying or pain, for the old order of things has passed away.
> (Revelation chapter 21 verse 4)

Chapter 10

POEM - LITTLE BIRD

Perched beside the ocean
    In a tree set way up high,
Sat a nest, held strong in branches,
      With four baby chicks inside.

The mother bird was very near
With food to satisfy.
The little chicks grew bigger
As each sunny day went by.

She gave her babies lessons,
She taught them wrong from right,
Then one day she had noticed
It was time to take their flight.

They had some practice take-offs
And flapped their brand new feathers.
One by one they had become
Well versed in all their measures.

And then the day arrived,
When the little ones should fly.
She knew it must be done
But mother bird still had a cry.

"Just remember, you've been given
Everything you need to fly.
You've got feathers, wings, direction
And you've even got good eyes.

Your landing gear is working
And your tail sits nice and high,
So, go on now and spread your wings
Soar up and reach the sky."

One little bird arranged his feathers,
Lifted up his chin,
He climbed up on the straw nest-edge
And gave his Mum a grin.

He summoned all his courage,
Suppressed those butterflies,
Took one more step, held his breath,
And then he shut his eyes.

The breeze swept up and caught his wings,
The bird was quite surprised.
It balanced and supported him,
It took him through the sky.

Across the town, across the school,
Across the meadows green,
He saw the blue horizon,
How the sun made waters gleam.

The little bird grew tired
And began to feel alone.
Very soon he swirled around
And headed on back home.

And when he saw his tree
Beside the ocean way up high,
He found his nest and came to rest,
And waved the breeze 'goodbye'.

"Oh, mother bird, we had such fun,
The breeze, the sky and I.
I'm glad you taught me very well,
I'm glad that I can fly."

Chapter 11

THE ISLAND THAT PRAYS TOGETHER, STAYS TOGETHER

The Island of Port Vila, Vanuatu was an adventure to visit. Kissed by the sun in the midst of winter, the locals were happy, and the water was sparkling. A beautiful sea playground and delight for snorkelers, its aqua coloured waters and natural settings were a treat for any who chose to pass that way.

It didn't take long though, to notice the effects of the recent category five cyclone that had devastated the island and its surrounds.

Our water-taxi driver was from the island of Ifira which is very close to Port Vila. As he ferried us around the outskirts of his island, we could see many fallen trees, smashed boats and roofless homes.

"That is our island's church," our driver said as he pointed to a church building prominently situated near the coast of Ifira and still in-tact. "It is a Presbyterian church. Everyone on our island goes to church and at the end of each day, we meet together in our family groups and have worship time."

"Everyone?" I questioned. Had I heard him correctly? He confirmed his answer quite adamantly. He continued to tell us about the cyclone as we pointed out the destroyed boats.

The island had been in direct line to the cyclone and, noticing how unsheltered it seemed to be, the journalist in me just had to probe a little: "Do you mind me asking how many fatalities you had from the cyclone?"

I was shocked to hear his answer was none!

"We had no fatalities on our island," he said. "We had some injuries but no fatalities. Everybody survived."

We were speechless. It didn't make any sense. From what we could see, this little unsheltered island didn't stand much of a chance.

Now having had time to look on the internet at the images of the cyclone, I am even more baffled as to how anyone could have survived such an incredibly powerful force.

I know bad things still happen to good people, there's no doubt about it and it's all part of the journey, but every now and then remarkable miracles occur, and I think to myself, *Ah yes! There is God reminding us again of His power.*

My thoughts went to the story of Elijah in 1 Kings chapter 19. Israel had deserted God for pagan idols and God's prophets had been killed. Elijah was the only one left and had fled for his life. God told him to:

> Go out and stand on the mountain in the presence of the Lord, for the Lord is about to pass by. (verse 11)

Anyone may well have thought that God was in the great and powerful wind which came and *'tore the mountains apart and shattered the rocks'* or in the earthquake that followed it. Or perhaps even that God was in the fire that came next (verse 11). But God was not in these.

After these disasters, there was a gentle whisper: the whisper of God. When Elijah heard this voice he knew to be God, he covered his face with his cloak, and went out and stood at the mouth of the cave. It was not God's intention to hurt Elijah, but to speak to him gently, giving him comfort and courage to go back and face what he had to do.

God showed the power of His great love by saving him supernaturally from things that, in the natural, would kill him. Through this, Elijah knew he had nothing to fear.

When I switch on the news and see the horrible things that the human race does to each other, I think it is amazing that even though God has the power to wipe us off the face of the earth, He chooses not to. Instead, He is gently calling us back to Him.

In all His grace, He continues to pursue us. Even though, *'since the creation of the world God's invisible qualities – his eternal power and divine nature – have been clearly seen, being understood from what has been made, so that people are without excuse' (Romans chapter 1, verse 20)*, people still continue to reject Him. Yet, in His great love, He is graciously giving us time to come back to Him.

The people of Ifira still worship together. They know the One who is their rock and their shelter, and in this, their faith is found.

> You have been a refuge for the poor, a refuge for the needy in their distress, a shelter from the storm and a shade from the heat.
>
> (Isaiah chapter 25, verse 4)

Chapter 12

THE THING ABOUT THAT GOAT

We have a pet goat called Bono and a sheep called Raphi. We've had them since they were babies. They're pretty cute and on a good day they graze on the hill which creates a peaceful scene for us to gaze upon from our lounge-room windows.

At most other times, however, Bono the goat gets up to mischief.

For our goat, the grass is always greener on the other side. Although we have a large piece of land for our animals to graze, it seems Bono has a knack for escaping, literally pushing the boundaries.

He wants more, so in a single bound, Bono is able to leap over gates, push down barriers and escape from harnesses. This is especially difficult when new concrete has been laid, hence to say, our new driveway is now permanently embossed with Bono's escape hoof tracks!

Bono spends much time looking for trouble. He finds the highest areas and elevates himself to any new platform he finds, even if it includes the roof of my car. His favourite foods are straw gardening hats, fruit trees and new plants.

He likes to find the closest dirt hill to roll down after a bath and is always on the lookout for an open door to the house, once bolting through a piano lesson only to run into the closed glass door at the other end of the room.

Now Raphi the sheep, on the other hand, is lovely. While there is no one outside, Raphi stays close to Bono. Sometimes Bono leads him astray and they escape together. Other times Raphi will sound the alarm when Bono has escaped or if there is a perceived danger.

When Tony or I are in the yard with them, Raphi doesn't leave our side. He knows who his masters are, he knows our voice. He will follow us wherever we go. He looks out for his friend Bono and tries to warn him or us when help is needed. His desire is to be close to us, his masters, and he trusts that we will provide what he needs on the land that we have given him.

Bono is always on the lookout for the next bit of trouble he can find. He is stubborn and when he doesn't want to go somewhere, he will drop his legs and make us carry him or push him the entire way.

Whereas Raphi is happy to follow and seems largely content. He heeds warnings, is cautious, looks out for his friend and, although Bono and Raphi literally butt heads, Raphi the sheep is an ever constant, loyal companion to Bono the goat.

The different nature of these animals is so striking that I often think about the Bible references to sheep and goats.

Sheep vs. Goat
In Matthew chapter 25, verses 31–46, Jesus tells a parable about sheep and goats. If you're not familiar with the story, here is a quick rundown. Basically, Jesus talks of judgment day. He explains how God will separate the sheep on His right and the goats on His left.

He calls the sheep blessed for they gave food to the hungry, drink to the thirsty, cared for strangers, and visited those who were sick and in prison. Jesus tells them that it was as if they had done these things for Him. To these sheep, He promises a kingdom prepared for them since the creation of the world.

Now, I know we can't work our way to heaven, but I guess if we look at this example closely, the kind of heart required to be of this nature would be one of love, compassion, empathy, and selflessness.

The goats, however, did not look after others. They did not give food to the hungry, drink to the thirsty, care for a stranger, or clothes to those who needed it. They did not visit the sick or those in prison.

The kind of heart required to be of this nature would be one of thoughtlessness, stubbornness, self-centredness, self-gain, self-promotion, and self-seeking. In fact, their world revolves around 'self', subsequently at the cost of others.

The heart of God
I love this passage because what we are seeing here is a mirror of God's own heart. He loves His creation and knows that we are more than capable of looking after each other. His heart breaks when we don't because it causes unnecessary pain.

Just as I am pleased with Raphi when I see him looking out for his friend, God is overjoyed when He sees His children serving others and caring for those in need. He doesn't ask us to do anything He wouldn't do Himself.

He gave the ultimate example; lowering Himself to the lowest of circumstances when He came to the earth and sacrificed His life to save us, breaking the bonds of death in His resurrection. He longs to draw us near to Him so much that His love knows no bounds.

If we can share that same love with others, then we are sharing His heart and maybe, giving others a glimpse of Jesus too.

> Sitting down, Jesus called the Twelve and said, "Anyone who wants to be first must be the very last, and the servant of all."
>
> (Mark chapter 9, verse 35)

Chapter 13

SHINE BRIGHT LIKE A DIAMOND

Ten thousand women packed the Qantas Stadium in Sydney for a weekend in March. Most men would have run for the hills! But this conference for women was special, touching the hearts of most, if not every woman there.

As I listened to the speakers, I was touched by their candour, their honesty and their courage.

Although these were very successful people, they spoke from their darkest times. Some have come through those times into better situations, and others are still in the midst of hard times and spoke of the daily strength they are receiving to step through each moment.

None of these stories were easy to tell. They came from brokenness and total surrender. But power was in their testimony and that's what cut through to the heart of the listener.

Revelation chapter 12 verses 10–11 says:

> For the accuser of our brothers and sisters, who accuses them before our God day and night, has been hurled down. They triumphed over him by the blood of the Lamb and by the word of their testimony.

There is power in the testimony
Each and every person has a story whether they know it or not.

Throwing my gaze across the sea of women, I was struck to think of the stories each one brought with them. Stories of pain, heartache, joy, and love. The places and situations they came from, the turmoil they may have endured, the challenges they have overcome. Some would return to homes of love, and some would return to homes of emptiness or challenge.

I think women are pretty amazing (men are too of course – some of my favourite people are men but for the sake of this article I will address my thoughts on women).

Whenever a group of women get together, you just have to mention 'childbirth' and stories of surviving extreme life and death experiences emerge. Bring up a topic on sickness and you will hear of trials, pain, and miracles.

Bring up the topic of children and you will see straight to the heart of many women. Bring up the topic of life in the workforce and you will hear stories of strength, endurance and overcoming.

I have seen friends get knocked down repeatedly, suffer physical challenges day in, day out. I see them carry heart-burdens for their friends and family to help carry the load, and I see some wrestle to keep their households together – though they are knocked down, they rise up again and again to face another day.

These women are heroes in my eyes and make me proud to be a woman.

Sometimes we feel like there is not a lot going on, but God is leading us to a destination and one day we will look back and see there was purpose in it all.

Most of us have been through, are going through, or will go through times that shape, mould and renew us, and one day we will emerge refined, shining bright like diamonds.

> But he knows the way that I take; when he has tested me, I will come forth as gold.
> (Job chapter 23 verse 10)

Chapter 14

STOP!
IT'S COFFEE TIME

O kay busy mums: it's time for a coffee break. Put away what you're doing and take a breather.

You've made it to the end of another busy day. Yes, it was a great feat in organisation. Clothes were washed, children were delivered to activities, meals were made, floors were cleaned, bills were paid, shopping was done, work was completed and now the children are all back where they should be, and you didn't forget anyone ... phew! Well done.

Sometimes you feel tired, but you do what you do because you love them, and you'll do it again tomorrow, and the next day, and the day after that.

Sometimes you run yourself ragged and yet, your efforts may have gone unnoticed. But that's okay too. You don't seem to mind because you're just glad they're happy.

You are doing a great job
You're juggling many things and yet it's working. Celebrate that. You are caring for your family and that's important.

> Truly I tell you, whatever you did for one of the least of these brothers and sisters of mine, you did for me.
> (Matthew chapter 25, verse 40)

Sometimes though, things don't always go to plan. You know you're not perfect, nobody is, but you're giving it all you've got and that's all you can give. No one expects more than that.

What you do may seem insignificant to others. That's not for you to worry about. The Bible says that you are honoured:

> She watches over the affairs of her household ... Honour her for all that her hands have done and let her works bring her praise at the city gate.
> (Proverbs chapter 31, verses 27-31)

You're looking after His little ones. You're loving those God has given to you. You are exercising the greatest power known to man.

> The greatest of these is love.
> (1 Corinthians chapter 13, verse 13)

You've given up your own desires for the needs of others and yes, you're probably going to have to do it all again tomorrow.

> For even the Son of Man did not come to be served but to serve, and to give his life as a ransom for many.
> (Mark chapter 10, verse 45)

The world of your family would be a very different place if you weren't doing what you're doing – loving them. So, keep doing it. They may or may not see your full worth, but remember you are precious in the eyes of God and He sees you. He knows.

> You are the God who sees me.
> (Genesis chapter 16, verse 13)

He loves those you care for
They too are His children, and He knows He can trust you with them, that's why He gave them to you. He's also there to help you.

> He gathers the lambs in his arms and carries them close to his heart; he gently leads those that have young.
> (Isaiah chapter 40, verse 11)

He will not forget you, for just as you are giving of your life to serve others, He gave the ultimate price – His life – to serve you.

> I will not forget you! See, I have engraved you on the palms of my hands.
> (Isaiah chapter 49, verses 15-16)

So now, as you settle in for some sleep, although it be in short bursts for those of you with waking babies, you can close your eyes and:

> Let the beloved of the Lord rest secure in him, for he shields him all day long, and the one the Lord loves rests between his shoulders.
> (Deuteronomy chapter 33, verse 12)

Chapter 15

SO ... WHAT HOPE DO WE HAVE?

Someone recently asked me, "If there was one verse in the Bible you could give to your children to remember, what would it be?"

Well, I thought about this and decided that there were just so many to choose from. The Bible as a whole gives the best picture of God's wonderful love for us and what it took to save us from ourselves.

There is the obvious verse from John chapter 3 verse 16:

> For God so loved the world that he gave his one and only son that whoever believes in him shall not perish but have eternal life.

'Perish', a word that distinctly describes where our world looks like it is heading, and this concerns me for the sake of future generations.

> For the wages of sin is death, but the gift of
> God is eternal life in Jesus Christ our Lord.
> (Romans chapter 6 verse 23)

Some days, after listening to the news, I feel so downhearted, and I know many others do too. The world is in a mess, and I wonder what our world is going to look like for our children and their children to come. What will primary school and secondary school education look like in the future? What will public advertising look like in the future? With bombings, senseless killings, and countless controversial issues, it is not a time to fall in a heap and just accept things the way they are.

God cherishes the heart of those who mourn over the evil things that are done in this world. In Ezekiel chapter 9 verse 4, the Lord says:

> Go throughout the city of Jerusalem and put
> a mark on those who grieve and lament over
> all the detestable things that are done in it.

These people were kept safe in an hour of terror.

I love my future descendants even though they are not yet born, and I want this world to be a better place for them. Call me old fashioned, that's okay and nothing to be ashamed of, but I want schools and society to largely reflect the same set of values that I have been brought up with in my Christian faith.

Unfortunately, Christian opinions and beliefs are often scorned at, belittled and tossed aside even though it is these morals, where followed, that are the backbone to creating a good and healthy society for generations to come because that's why God, in all His wisdom, ordained them.

Scripture portions poignant
In Psalm chapter 119 it seems David was feeling the same way.

> "Though rulers sit together and slander me," he says, "your servant will meditate on your decrees." (verse 23)

Of course, there are many who call themselves Christians who, without remorse, have also committed atrocities either out of selfish gain or in the name of their faith. But that doesn't discount those who have a heart to follow the Word of God, especially knowing that they themselves are sinners and that God has saved them from a path that will lead to destruction.

We know that by no means is anyone without sin.

> There is no difference, for all have sinned and fall short of the glory of God, and are justified freely by his grace through the redemption that came by Christ Jesus.
> (Romans chapter 3 verses 22-24)

Jesus socialised with those the world despised, tax collectors, prostitutes, adulterers etc. yet He did not conform to their ways, or lobby to change the laws of the land to allow their behaviour, instead He said to one adulterer, *"go now and leave your life of sin,"* (John chapter 8 verse 11).

Because of His great love, He then paid the price for her and everyone else when He died on the cross.

God meets us where we are whatever shape we are in, and He loves us. But once we have 'met' with Him, we cannot help but be changed. When we have truly 'met' with him, we want to put away our old selves and go and sin no more. We are changed just like the adulterer was.

> Do we, then, nullify the law by this faith? Not at all! Rather, we uphold the law.
> (Romans chapter 3 verse 31)

We are not to compromise our faith for popularity.

> If you do not stand firm in your faith, you will not stand at all.
> (Isaiah chapter 7 verse 9)

We need to keep our saltiness
Romans chapter 12 verse 9 says to, *"Hate what is evil; cling to what is good."* Notice it says hate *what* is evil, not *who*.

So, what are we to do? Jesus says:

> But I tell you who hear me: Love your enemies, do good to those who hate you, bless those who curse you, pray for those who mistreat you.
> (Luke chapter 6 verses 27-28)

> ... if your enemy is hungry, feed him; if he is thirsty, give him something to drink.
> (Romans chapter 12 verse 20)

God's love unconditional
I know, it goes against our initial response, but God asks us to love the person without accepting the behaviour. Jesus says:

> If you love those who love you, what credit is that to you? Even 'sinners' love those who love them.
> (Luke chapter 6 verse 32)

Therefore, we have to step out of ourselves and love without compromising our faith.

> And now these three remain: faith, hope and love. But the greatest of these is love.
>
> (1 Corinthians chapter 13 verse 13)

So, if you asked me what verse I would give to my children in this day, I would say Jeremiah chapter 29 verse 11:

> "For I know the plans I have for you," declares the Lord, "plans to prosper you and not to harm you, plans to give you hope and a future."

For God does not give us rules to spoil our fun. They are there to protect us individually and collectively as a human race because He loves what He has made, and so that we may enjoy life in *'all its fullness'*.

I would tell them that their Father in Heaven has the best plan for their lives and to love His precepts and that regardless of what the world does – God is still God, and always will be even long after we've left this earth.

> Acknowledge and take to heart this day that the Lord is God in heaven above and on the earth below. There is no other.
>
> (Deuteronomy chapter 4 verses 38-40)

Chapter 16

GUESS HOW MUCH I LOVE YOU?

Being thankful in all circumstances can sometimes be challenging. Within 48 hours we ran out of tank water, had an eight-hour power outage and to top it off, a magpie flew into my house and pooped all over my floor, lounge, and curtains.

Frustrating? By all means! But so ridiculous that I had to laugh, especially when I found the bird in my house.

At first it was hard to find something to be thankful for but soon I was grateful that we were able to have water delivered to replenish the empty tank, the power eventually came back on, and the magpie pooped before I washed the floor and not after. And really, it wasn't detrimental, only inconvenient for a very short time in the grand scheme of things.

In the rush to the end of the year, it can be challenging to pause to be thankful, but reflection is important.

The last few weeks of the term have seen the culmination of the year's activities, the celebrations of achievements, the end of one era and thoughts of an upcoming new one.

In amongst the busyness of it all, some lovely American friends of ours invited us to share their traditional Thanksgiving dinner with *all the fixin's*. It was a time to pause and reflect. The table was traditionally decorated and laden with a banquet of delicious turkey, stuffing, green bean casserole, salads and pecan and pumpkin pies. My friend had done an amazing job.

I was struck at what a beautiful tradition it is and how lovely it was to be sitting with family and friends, taking time out to thank God for each other and for the gifts He has given us throughout the year.

During conversation, thanks were given for God's provision and the precious gift of family, friends and people in our lives who have shared the year with us. These are gifts that live in our hearts and endure throughout the years.

People make us better people; friends make us better friends; and family help us to feel the belonging that God wants us to feel with Him.

Reflection

I sit here now as rain pours from the sky. My tanks are filling and so are those of all my neighbours. I love that God gives gifts to everyone whether they know Him or not, whether they realise it or not.

Babies are born every minute – a gift from God. Rain falls from the sky – a gift from God. Plants grow so that we can eat – a gift from God. Beautiful sunsets grace evening skies – a gift from God. Even the diversion on our path that keeps us from harm – a gift from God and so it goes.

James chapter 1 verse 17 says:

> Every good and perfect gift is from above, coming down from the Father of the heavenly lights, who does not change like shifting shadows.

Perhaps God is trying to get our attention and, though we may be too busy to stop and say thank you or even acknowledge The Creator, He still gives.

Following thanksgiving, we turn our focus to Christmas with all its glitter and festivities. I am especially thankful for the gift of God's son Jesus, who came into the world not to stone or condemn the sinner, but to pay the price for them and welcome us into His home.

I love this Dr Seuss quote:

> *"And the Grinch, with his Grinch-feet ice cold in the snow,*
> *stood puzzling and puzzling, how could it be so?*
> *It came without ribbons. It came without tags.*
> *It came without packages, boxes or bags.*
> *And he puzzled and puzzled 'till his puzzler was sore.*
> *Then the Grinch thought of something he hadn't before.*
> *What if Christmas, he thought, doesn't come from a store.*
> *What if Christmas, perhaps, means a little bit more."*
>
> (Dr. Seuss, How the Grinch Stole Christmas)

Perhaps Christmas does mean a little bit more – a whole lot more. Hopefully we can take the gifts God gives us and of His Son and thank Him throughout the whole year.

Chapter 17

LIFE, PARENTING AND YAPPING ANKLE-BITERS

As soon as a baby takes its first breath, it is wholly reliant on others to keep it alive. Whether a child makes it to birth, lives only a few hours or a lifetime, there is a purpose for that child to be here, it is a gift to be treasured.

With life comes trials, pain and heartache but along with the tough stuff there are so many moments of love, joy and belly-aching hilarity that must be enjoyed and savoured.

Parenting is a steep learning curve of unselfishness. Before I had children, my life was my own. I could do as I pleased, go where I pleased, eat what I pleased – you get the idea. But as soon as my first child was born, that all went out the window. My world became focussed on what was best for my child and later, my children.

Not only have I given them my time and focus but I feel every emotion with them. I hurt when they hurt, I laugh when they laugh, I feel their anger, I share their frustrations and their disappointments. We are forever connected. Sometimes the pain can be great, and I wonder how God, the Father of all, handles the heartache of so many children.

I often think how God's heart must break time and time again. When He sees His creation conspire, deceive, and fight against each other. When they kill, steal, destroy, and torture. It is so sad.

But to think of God's enormous capacity to love and how great God's love is, His heart must be enormously strong to handle how painfully it must break every time He sees a little one of His hurt by violence, innocence stolen, children torn from their parents, trafficked and the list goes on. It is almost too unbearable to think about. I don't know these children personally, but God does.

Mums may carry their children for a time, but God created them and carries them for eternity. He knit them together in their mother's womb, He knew them before they were born, He knows how many hairs are on their heads, He knows all the days of their lives. But there is sin in the world and when people use their gift of free will to abuse and hurt others, it pains Him – oh how it pains Him!

Is He just sitting back and letting it happen? Certainly not! In Deuteronomy chapter 32 verse 36, God says:

> Have I not kept this in reserve and sealed it in my vaults? It is mine to avenge; I will repay. In due time their foot will slip; their day of disaster is near and their doom rushes upon them.

And again, in Luke chapter 17 verse 2:

> It would be better for them to be thrown into the sea with a millstone tied around their neck than to cause one of these little ones to stumble.

Imagining

I can imagine God's anger would be of thunder-rolling, lightning-striking, earth-cracking biblical proportions. But His pain is not just for those who have suffered at the hands of perpetrators; it is also for the perpetrators.

Imagine receiving a puppy for Christmas. This puppy is loving and beautiful, the cutest thing you've ever seen. You take photos, post them to Facebook and take this puppy everywhere you go.

As the puppy grows, he starts to turn on you. He bites your ankles every time he sees you. He growls every time someone says your name. He starts attacking your other pets almost to the point of death. I think my heart would break.

To see this puppy that I loved so much turn against me would make me feel like he had missed out on so much goodness that had been stored up for him.

Would you just strike this puppy down straight away with no remorse? I don't think so. You would hope they would turn back and remember where they came from.

That is how God feels for His creation. He loves it because He carefully and purposely made it. He gives many, many warnings before He allows disaster to strike. He has told us through prophesies in the Bible what is to come and how to get back to Him. He even gave His own Son to die on the cross to pay for our mistakes to make it as easy as possible for us to come to Him. His heart aches for us to know Him. Yet He is rejected over and over again. For those who hear Him, He offers peace.

> Here I am! I stand at the door and knock. If anyone hears my voice and opens the door, I will come in and eat with that person, and they with me.
> (Revelation chapter 3 verse 20)

He is calling you – can you hear Him? Open the door and let Him in. He loves you.

Chapter 18

THREE WAYS TO HELP YOUR CHILDREN COPE WITH FEAR

Recently I had to give myself a good talking to. I was becoming overwhelmed with the amount of terror saturating my social media sites, on the news and in conversation.

The barbarism and evil that I was seeing, is so foreign and shocking to our way of life, that it concerned me as to how this would be affecting our children.

As mums, we are nesters. We like to know our children are safe and as soon as anything threatens that, we go into protective mode. Perhaps not so much of an issue for my younger children, as we don't often watch the nightly news, but my teenagers are well aware of social issues, and it is a burden they shouldn't have to carry alone.

I don't want them to be completely naive but there are certain things that we as parents can do to limit the amount of exposure our children have to this information and give them the right perspective on what they are exposed to.

1. Let joy be louder than fear
The greatest thing the enemy wants us to feel is fear, and the greatest weapon we have to fight fear with is joy. Keeping life as normal and fun as possible helps children to feel secure. The world around us may look very crazy but your home is your safe haven. That is the place where you get to keep control even when the world seems out of control.

Keep your conversation light and keep a good sense of humour. It might be a good idea to have a day or night of the week when you do something fun together as a family. You may already be doing this which is great! Keep doing it. Whether it is a picnic at the beach or watching a funny movie, family togetherness is an enjoyable way to relieve stress and is a great distractor from negative thoughts.

> Nehemiah said, "Go and enjoy choice food and sweet drinks, and send some to those who have nothing prepared. This day is holy to our Lord. Do not grieve, for the joy of the Lord is your strength."
> (Nehemiah chapter 8 verse 10)

2. Let hope light the way

Around the time of the 9/11 terrorist attacks on the Twin Towers, I remember hearing a quote by Fred Rogers:

> *When I was a boy and I would see scary things in the news, my mother would say to me, "Look for the helpers. You will always see people helping."*

He then went on to say:

> *... because if you look for the helpers, you'll know that there's hope.*

Hope

It is easy to be overwhelmed by evil but there is also so much good that should be acknowledged that we don't always hear about.

As a parent, depending on the situation, I sometimes find it more effective to reward the good behaviour and pay less attention to the bad. While the bad behaviour still needs to be dealt with, it is in the rewarding of the good behaviour that encourages and drives more good behaviour. It also gives the child a state of mind to pursue and identify goodness.

Whenever you see or hear a story of how an individual or group of people has done something to help victims and shown love, make it a point of conversation. Let that be the news article that gets the family's attention. Reward the good deeds of others by paying attention to them and that in turn brings hope to our own hearts.

> You answer us with awesome and righteous deeds, God our Saviour, the hope of all the ends of the earth and of the farthest seas.
> (Psalm chapter 65 verse 5)

3. Let wisdom be our guide

Reassure children that as their parents, you will do everything possible to keep them safe. We are their protectors and whilst we keep our children's minds from worry, we ourselves still need to be vigilant. Shutting our eyes and hoping it will just go away won't help anything.

Being aware of what is going on and being alert to what we can do to help others is important. When there is opportunity to give – give. When there is a need to pray – pray. When we need to speak – speak.

> ... and after you have done everything – to stand.
> (Ephesians chapter 6 verse 13)

Sometimes it feels easier to pretend it isn't happening. It may not be on our doorstep, or it may be, but either way we need to be wise in knowing what is going on, speaking up when necessary and guarding our hearts and our homes.

> Be alert, stand firm in the faith, be brave, be strong.
> (1 Corinthians chapter 16 verse 13)

Australian-American pop duo, For King and Country, sum it up well in their song 'Fix My Eyes':

> *I'd love like I'm not scared*
> *Give when it's not fair*
> *Live life for another*
> *Take time for a brother*
> *Fight for the weak ones*
> *Speak out for freedom*
> *Find faith in the battle*
> *Stand tall but above it all*
> *Fix my eyes on you*

When all is said and done, it is our Father in Heaven who keeps us safe and who watches over us, so therefore, our eyes are best kept on Him.

> Let the beloved of the Lord rest secure in him, for he shields him all day long, and the one the Lord loves rests between his shoulders.
> (Deuteronomy chapter 33 verse 12)

Chapter 19

DRESSED FOR SUCCESS

I don't normally drive in my pyjamas. In fact, it was the first time I'd ever done it. Apparently for some of my friends it's a regular occurrence but dropping my teenage daughter off at 6.15am for school camp in my pyjamas was not what I had in mind.

Yes, I could roll off the excuses like, 'I thought Tony was going to drive her, until the concreter turned up at the door when it was time to leave', but that doesn't change the fact that I wasn't prepared for what was needed.

As I drove, I prayed so hard that I wouldn't get pulled over by the police or that the car wouldn't break down before I got home. Thankfully my daughter thought it was funny (as it was her idea) and laughed about it even though I couldn't help get her luggage out of the car once we arrived at the bus.

Although my flannelette pyjamas were the epitome of comfort on a cold winter's day, it was not a feeling of comfort that I felt when I stepped out in public in them. My comfortable pyjamas actually restricted me from being of help to others and limited where I could go.

To be of help, I had to change. I had to put on the clothes that would equip me for the tasks ahead, whatever they may be.

There are many times in life that we miss opportunities because we are not prepared. Sometimes these are due to circumstances that are of no fault of our own and other times it is just a lack of motivation, organisation or even courage.

It is easy to get comfortable. We get into our familiar routines. Day in, day out we know largely what to expect. But sometimes being comfortable can be uncomfortable.

Sure, we may seem to have everything under control and life seems to be smooth sailing, but deep down there is a nagging that says, "Are you fulfilling the purpose that God has put you on the earth to do?" And although this may make you uncomfortable, finding your purpose brings its own rewards.

Touch of reality
Some people know what their talents are from an early age. For others they may seem hidden and need searching out. Writing a list of things you enjoy can be

helpful in identifying what your gifts are. Very soon a picture will develop of who you are and help point you in the right direction.

I did this exercise years ago when I was in the midst of nappies, baby food and prams. It proved to be a great re-focuser. I began to incorporate those strengths or 'gifts' into the stage of life that I was in at that time, which was being a stay-a-home Mum, a role I embraced with all my heart.

Amongst other things, I began writing stories to read to my children, I tried new recipes, I applied for courses, and made movies in our backyard with my children as the leading roles. This also fuelled their passions for all things creative (two of them later studying and working in filmmaking and media).

I realised that I didn't necessarily need to learn something new; instead, I needed to develop what I already had.

The training ground of those days was more important than I ever imagined at the time. As my children grow and my circles of influence increase, I find I am prepared to take on more than I otherwise would have been ready for if I hadn't identified the things I love.

The seemingly small things are anything but insignificant. Zechariah chapter 4 verse 10 says:

> Does anyone dare despise this day of small beginnings? They'll change their tune when they see Zerubbabel setting the last stone in place!

God has a plan for your life, and He has equipped you with everything you need to accomplish it. He foreknew you and predestined a purpose for your life, (Romans chapter 8 verse 29). So, if you truly believe that God:

> ... is able to do immeasurably more than all we ask or imagine, according to his power that is at work within us ...
> (Ephesians chapter 3 verse 20)

then maybe it's time to be brave and seek God's will for your life.

> May God ... who put you together, provide you with everything you need to please him, make us into what gives him most pleasure, by means of the sacrifice of Jesus, the Messiah.
> (Hebrews chapter 13 verses 21-22)

Chapter 20

POEM - LITTLE BOAT CALLED HOPE

The wind was rushing, the waves were crushing,
And high upon gusty seas,
The little boat came sailing,
Though nothing he could see.

'I know the land is near,' he said,
'It won't be far away.'
Though night was here,
He did not fear,
For morning would bring day.

And so, the boat kept sailing,
He knew he'd see the sun.
Standing firm and standing strong
Was all that could be done.

'Hello there,' said a wee small voice,
'I wonder if you'd mind,
I floated on a comfy log,
Which now I just can't find.'

'Well, come up here,
Rest in my boat, we'll sail together fine.
We'll sail until the morning comes.'
So, in hopped Mousie Tyne.

And on they sailed
Until one hailed
'I can swim not one more stroke!
I'm tired and I'm weary,
I can barely even float.'

'Well, come up here,
Rest in my boat,
We'll sail together well.
We'll sail until the morning comes.'
So, in hopped Bunny Belle.

So Mousie Tyne and Bunny Belle
Sailed in the little boat.
Though nothing could be seen by them
They did not give up hope.

'I see a light.
It is quite bright.
I think it is the sun!
As soon as we can reach the land,
Our sailing will be done!'

YOU COULD BE DANCING

And so, they sailed right to the sand,
To where the little boat could land
And in an instant, both were out
And Bunny could not help but spout:

'Oh, thank you little sailing boat,
Without you there would be no hope.
You saved us and we're very glad,
To stay out there would be quite mad!'

'My pleasure,' said the little boat,
'Just remember to take note,
That when it's dark and very glum,
Remember that the sun will come,
And that will get you through the night,
Just look and you will see a light.'

Chapter 21

WORDS FOR DINNER

As we were driving home from school recently, I was listening to my children sing with great fervour:

> *Let my words be life,*
> *let my words be truth.*
> *I don't want to say a word*
> *unless it points the world*
> *back to you.*
> ('Words' by Hawk Nelson)

It got me thinking how so often our words can sound anything but graceful.

Have you ever heard words come out of your mouth and thought, *Oh, that's not how it sounded in my head!* It can feel like a wall of bricks just fell out of the sky and landed on top of you.

If done regularly, it carries the title of foot-in-mouth disease – *'noun Informal: Facetious. the habit of making inappropriate, insensitive, or imprudent statements.'* (dictionary.com)

Winston Churchill once said,

> *'In the course of my life, I have often had to eat my words, and I must confess that I have always found it a wholesome diet.'*

Well, I'm not sure about the 'wholesome diet', but it is something that people have been grappling with right throughout the course of history.

Words can do a lot of damage even if the intention was not to do so. They can tear people down, they can damage dreams, they can hurt right to the core, they can shatter people.

On the flip side however, how wonderful it is when the right words are said at the right time. They can bring hope and healing, they can motivate, encourage and give life.

> A person finds joy in giving an apt reply –
> and how good is a timely word.
> (Proverbs chapter 15 verse 23)

Everywhere we go, there are people who need words of hope. The gift of the right word at the right time and a listening ear can be a breath of life in an unrelenting world.

John 1 verses 1-4 says:

> In the beginning was the Word, and the Word was with God, and the Word was God. He was with God in the beginning. Through him all things were made; without him nothing was made that has been made. In him was life, and that life was the light of all mankind. The light shines in the darkness, and the darkness has not overcome it.

As the world gets darker, let your light shine brighter and may the words you say bring life, hope and healing, drawing people closer to the light of God, the hope of the world.

Chapter 22

LIST MAKERS, RELAX!

Hands up if you are a list-maker! I gather there are quite a few of us out there.

Don't you love the feeling of when a plan comes together? You have made the list, set out the program, planned the date and everything is going according to plan. You are loving the feeling of being organised, in control and self-sufficient. Yep, you don't need any help because you've got it all sorted.

Then the antagonist 'spanner-in-the-works' pays you a visit and the clogs get jammed, the planning comes undone, and nothing is completed or falls into place the way it is supposed to.

I've had that happen far too many times and though my best laid plans seemed to be faultless, that's when the car would break down, or it would rain on the outdoor birthday party, or the shop had run out of that one last piece that would make everything fit into place.

So often, it is also easy to look at the coming week and wonder how we'll ever do it. How we'll get through the long list of demands and pressing appointments, as well as organising our children's social lives and events and accomplish everything that must get done.

If we look too far outside of the day that we are in, it can be overwhelming. Our heart rate increases, and our minds begin to scroll through times and dates, how-to's and deadlines.

It is then we need to take our thoughts captive and put our focus back onto God. He is waiting for us to lean into Him. He doesn't want us to worry about the future because that is when we miss out on the present.

He has given us grace for each day. He walks with us in the present and says:

> Don't worry about tomorrow for tomorrow will bring its own troubles. Today's troubles are enough for today.
>
> (Matthew chapter 6 verse 34)

Just like the Israelites in the Old Testament had only enough manna for each day, so God will give us what we need for each day if we trust in Him.

These days I tend not to make so many lists. Learning that I haven't always got the answers, that I can't predict every step that I will take during a day, and that I don't have the super powers required to enable me to control the actions of others has a way of helping me to surrender to the One who does know my steps before I take them and who does know what I need before I even ask.

When we focus on Him and let Him take the reins, we can relax and know that we are in good hands, the best.

> You will keep him in perfect peace, whose mind is stayed on You, because he trusts in You.
> (Isaiah chapter 26 verse 3)

So, the next time you make a list, hold it loosely and let The One who loves you most, direct your paths and your lists according to His purposes.

> Many are the plans in a person's heart, but it is the Lord's purpose that prevails.
> (Proverbs chapter 19 verse 21)

Chapter 23

EVERY THREAD COUNTS

When I fell pregnant with my first baby, I wanted to give her a gift. I chose a very cute teddy bear cross-stitch pattern, bought the required threads, needles, and accessories, and began to stitch.

By the end of my pregnancy, I had finished my project. What began as a few threads of tiny, coloured crosses on my fabric, ended up to be just as the picture on the front of the pattern revealed. I proudly hung it in a timber frame above the cot that was awaiting the arrival of my baby girl.

With all good intentions, when I fell pregnant with my second baby, I also wanted to give him a gift. So off I went and found a very cute cross-stitch, roughly the same size as the first, and bought all of the threads and accessories that I needed to complete the work.

What I didn't realise however, was that feeding, changing nappies and washing had now filled in the time I used to have for 'projects', and this particular cross-stitch is still, many years later, a work in progress. Babies number three and four will receive a cross-stitch at some point in their lives but it may be on the birth of their own children at this rate.

Shameful, I know, but as many mums out there can relate, once children enter the scene, 'projects' tend to wedge their way down the list of priorities.

Did I take on more than I could chew? Perhaps. Perhaps a smaller sized cross-stitch would have made more sense. Or perhaps I got distracted. Nevertheless, I have seen the 'big picture' so to say, and I won't give up until it is finished.

Ah, some of you wise readers out there have picked up that I may not be talking only about cross-stitch now. Well, you're right.

In 1 Corinthians chapter 9 verses 24-27, Paul talks about running a race to reach the prize, a prize that will last forever. Then in Hebrews the author speaks of Jesus:

> ... the author and perfecter of our faith, who for the joy set before him endured the cross, scorning its shame, and sat down at the right hand of the throne of God.
>
> (chapter 12 verse 2)

It is easier to begin something if you can see what the outcome will be. Life is rarely like that. Sometimes it is very difficult to see why certain things happen or what point they have. They are, if you like, similar to working one colour of a cross-stitch. It just looks like thread on a fabric with no real design or shape.

1 Corinthians chapter 13 verse 12 says:

> For now we see through a glass, darkly; but
> then face to face: now I know in part; but
> then shall I know even as also I am known.

There is a bigger picture, one that makes sense and is beautiful to look at.

Although we don't fully understand what each thread of our life looks like in the bigger picture, we can trust that God has a design that is more beautiful than anything we have ever seen or imagined, and every thread counts. Without each colour sewn into the correct square, the picture makes no sense.

I'm so glad that when the picture of life seems to make little sense, there is a bigger picture that has been carefully designed by our Saviour.

> ... let us not become weary in doing good,
> for at the proper time we will reap a harvest
> if we do not give up.
>
> (Galatians chapter 6 verse 9)

Chapter 24

NO TIME FOR ACCUSATIONS

Can you hear it? That nag-nag-nagging?
"You can't do that," it says. "You're not good enough. You'll never be able to accomplish what you set out to do so why try? Just give up now."

Bullying is one of my pet-hates. Whether it is in a school yard, one sibling to another, or an adult bullying a child, teenager, or another adult – it is just not on. We see big businesses bullying smaller ones out of existence. We see those with money bully those without.

But have you ever heard the bullying in your own mind? The little voice inside your head that puts you down, like a hammer hitting against the head of the nail, thump-thump-thump. Each and every strike aimed at burying your courage just that little bit more, shrinking you down so that only a small shadow of yourself remains.

With the passing of grandparents in the last few years, one quite recently, I have been reflecting on life and how quickly it passes us by. The older I get, the faster the years seem to fly by. The age I thought was really old as a child, doesn't seem that old to me now. What I've come to realise is, that even though days can seem long, years are very short, and we need to make the most of our time here.

One of the most effective ways the devil gets us off-track from the purpose God put us here on the earth, is to decrease our value in our own eyes. He wants to cause damage by dismantling the creation God carefully put together to display His glory, and we listen to it! But we don't have time for that.

His plan
God has a plan for each and every one of us. He carefully created us and knows us from the most intricate detail of our souls to the most obvious. He knows what we are capable of, and He knows what was placed inside of us to be used for His glory.

He orders our days to meet the people we do at the specific times we meet them. He has given us individual talents and gifts that, if only we developed them and were brave enough to use them, they would be a blessing to others.

If we believe the lies the devil tells us, that we are not good enough, then we are further away from living the life that God had pre-ordained for us, and we lose our effectiveness and potential.

> Your eyes saw my unformed body; all the days ordained for me were written in your book before one of them came to be.
> (Psalm chapter 139 verse 16)

It is as though the nails that were hammered into Jesus hands were the accusations that we listen to in our heads. The devil thought he had won. With each strike that hammered the nails into Jesus' hands, Jesus took the weight of those accusations, pain, and sin, then when it seemed there was no life left, Jesus did something miraculous. He spectacularly broke the power of sin that led to death and triumphantly turned it into eternal life, breaking the chains of sin and death for all those who believe in Him.

> Then I heard a loud voice in heaven say: 'Now have come the salvation and the power and the kingdom of our God, and the authority of his Messiah. For the accuser of our brothers and sisters, who accuses them before our God day and night, has been hurled down. They triumphed over him by the blood of the Lamb and by the word of

> their testimony; they did not love their lives
> so much as to shrink from death.'
> > (Revelation chapter 12 verses 10-11)

His promises

Therefore, we need to become brave and stand on the truth that Jesus has paid the price for us and there is no condemnation for those who are in Christ (Romans chapter 8 verse 1). We need to hold on to the promises of God and stand on the truth of His word. And even though we will have to dodge metaphorical flaming arrows that are hurled at us every day, we will keep going.

> In addition to all this, take up the shield of faith, with which you can extinguish all the flaming arrows of the evil one.
> > (Ephesians chapter 6 verse 16)

When it all comes down to it, we don't have time to doubt ourselves. We need to focus on others and be available for God to use us wherever we are. As singer/songwriter Jason Gray says, *"God put a million, million doors in this world for his love to walk through. One of those doors is you."* (from song - With Every Act of Love)

Chances are, where you are feeling the accusations most strongly, that could be where God is using you most strongly. Be brave ...

Chapter 25

ARE WE THERE YET?

Have you ever had a plan for life or something you really felt was God's plan for your life? We dream, plan, design, act and work towards this end, and hope that one day it will be so.

Well, sometimes things just don't turn out the way we plan.

Years ago, after getting through some tough beginning years, we got to a place where all our ducks were in a row, so to speak. Several years prior we had finished the restoration of our home where we enjoyed entertaining family and friends. We were growing our four beautiful children and my husband's business was a success. He had finished his university degrees for a career change and received news that he had landed a well-paying, good solid government job in our dream location.

This meant that our plan of a sea change to raise our children, build our dream house, and live our dream life was beginning to take flight.

We sold our house, found a temporary rental, and purchased acreage on a mountain (20 minutes from the beach). We then completed our house design and sent the plans off to council for approval.

So, after some earlier health, financial struggles and setbacks, life was back on track, and we? Well, we were on top of the world. Things had finally fallen into place for us. We had no debts, a small fortune in the bank, the kids were newly settled and happy, and we were excited about this new stage of our life.

But you're waiting for it aren't you, that ominous 'but'? Well, here it is.

The five years that were to follow, did not go as we had planned. But rather a series of unfortunate events began to direct our path. The house that was to take six months to build, took over four years just for approval. The pre-approved loan was revoked and disappeared following the Global Financial Crisis, along with our 'invested' life saving. The job? Well, that is a story all of its own, but suffice to say, it was gone too and subsequently, no amount of university degrees, skills, experience or qualifications seemed to elicit another. In its place we received illness, hardship, more hardship, and more pain.

Stretched beyond the unthinkable

During that time, we were stretched beyond the unthinkable, strained beyond the thought of our limits, forced to learn to receive, and humbled to let others give.

Whatever we thought we could endure, we were wrong, very wrong. At one point we were under enormous pressure, the most pressure we had ever been under. We then had the bank ring to tell us they were foreclosing on a block of land that we couldn't sell or build on. It was so bad, that all we could say for comfort was, "Well, at least it can't get any worse."

Then it did. The following week I was involved in a serious head-on collision which brought with it a whole new set of problems, injury, and loss of a capacity to work which added further financial loss and expense.

In all these things and many times, we wondered why, pleading with God, and wrestling to understand where God was in this, why these things kept happening to us, and for so long. We would cry out to God to take away or change our circumstances for the better, but in return we received more and more trials taking us to the extreme edge of what we thought we could handle, and then beyond.

However, this is not a sob story. This is a story of trust, faith, and ultimately, triumph.

You see, what life brought our way to destroy us, ultimately only made us stronger, both as a family and as a couple. It seems that what we thought was best for us only got in the way of the 'better' that God had lovingly prepared for us and took great care to guide us through.

My husband would often quote the Scriptures, *"Though he slay us we will trust in him"* for if *"this is the day that God has made for us we must rejoice and be glad in it"* regardless! (paraphrased from Job 13:15 and Psalm 118:24)

It took years before we got to a point of obvious recovery. We continued to carry the wounds from the journey for some time, our income remained low and uncertain, and we had to take up people's offers to help pay basic bills at times. Our house was built, but almost completely by our own hands and not financed by a bank. We even had to move in with our parents for many months to get us over the line.

But though we were far from the life *we* had planned for ourselves; we were exactly in the plan that God had for us. God knew what He was doing, and thank God for that.

A life in God is not about us or our plans for our lives, but about God's unfailing love for us. It is God who directs our path and fashions us fit for His purpose. For if we truly are His, our faith and trust must remain in Him who is faithful. God is faithful. No matter how many times we fall, no matter how many things go wrong, God is in control and His glory will see us through to triumph.

We need to challenge ourselves
What if the restoration and healing is nothing to do with the situational or physical, but that the restoration and healing is of our minds and thoughts to trust God, despite the situational or physical circumstances?

What if the refinement He seeks for us is a total surrender to God's will, and the triumph – peace? Maybe life is about a journey of complete letting go and allowing God, who is your creator and lover of your soul, to walk you through this life like a parent leads a child.

Jesus reminds us:

> These things I have spoken to you, so that in Me you may have peace. For in this world you will have tribulation, but take courage; I have overcome the world.
> (John chapter 16 verse 33)

Our destination is not a house or place, our purpose is not a job, our life is not a living. It's all a journey which began long before we realised it. It's a journey that leads us back to God.

So, we trust in the Lord with all our heart, rejecting the tendency to lean on our own understandings, but instead, in all our ways, circumstances and situations, we acknowledge Him, and He makes our path back to Him, straight (paraphrased from Proverbs chapter 3 verses 5-6).

Our hope is in Him
God is faithful, constant, and purposeful. He has been with us every step of the way. Nothing goes to waste and though the journey is not finished, we understand that the work God had begun in us has to be completed for His glory and not for ours.

Looking back at our situation, we don't see the adversity was set to harm us but was a lovingly set path to refine us and those around us to be and act more like Jesus. Even now, as was then, we look around and we see people walking in the nature and heart of God, showing love, kindness, providing peace and comfort in, not just our situation, but also in theirs.

A whole different outlook
It's in sharing life's pains, successes and failures that centres our lives around a God who waits patiently for us, knocking gently at the door of our hearts, orchestrating situations and events to draw us together, giving us opportunity after opportunity to know Him.

During our trials and through our wrestling, it goes without saying that God is God. He is constant, He does not depend on the resources of the world to look after us, He will not leave us, He will not abandon us. He will deliver us.

Ultimately, God's ways are not our ways and submission to Him is the pathway to a place of peace even though we may look like fools to onlookers.

God is our provider, our comfort, our hope, and our healer. We have seen Him deliver the impossible, move the immoveable and light the path and our feet. We have seen hearts be moved and hands that help. We have seen God in the faces of our friends and family and occasionally strangers. We have been blessed.

> But he said to me, "My grace is sufficient for you, for my power is made perfect in weakness."
> (2 Corinthians chapter 12 verse 9)

When all is stripped away, God becomes very visible
Although I cannot compare our situation on a biblical scale, I draw great comfort from the stories of people in the Bible who have journeyed hard roads and endured: Jacob who wrestled with God, Joseph who was abandoned and sold by his brothers, Job who persevered through terrible adversities, and the list goes on. I am hopeful too when I read, that these stories had good outcomes.

So, having watched my husband build our house from morning till evening with his own hands the very house that now is our family home – it stands as a monument and reminder to hold onto the hope that God is faithful and always will be.

(Acknowledgement to my husband Tony, for his contribution to this chapter)

Chapter 26

ONE, TWO, THREE ...
LOOK AT ME

While leading Kids Church one Sunday, it was time to settle the children down from lively singing and birthday announcements to the more sedate mood of story time. With so much chatter going on, I had to think quick to retrieve their attention.

Suddenly I remembered a rhyme that my 'teacher' sister-in-law had joked about and so I blurted it through the microphone, "One, two, three...look at me."

Not being a schoolteacher myself, I didn't realise that this rhyme came with a response, and I was flabbergasted when there was immediate silence, all eyes to the front and then, as if in a conducted choir they replied in perfect unison, "One, two...eyes on you."

Wow! I was so impressed. I felt like I had a supernatural power. *I'll be using that one again,* I thought to myself.

Although I do my best to give my children the most attention that I can, I have noticed that they have their own 'special' language of getting my eyes onto them. As toddlers, it often came in the form of mischief: pegs down the toilet, artwork on the walls, baby cream in the carpet, and escaping over the fence, just to name a few.

But I think the one that works the best when I am distracted is repeating the name 'Mum' over and over and over again, enough to grate on anyone's nerves.

I've been thinking about this in regard to God. How does He get our eyes onto Him?

In Matthew chapter 14, Jesus walked on the water to meet the disciples in the boat. The waves were up, and the wind was against it. The disciples were terrified, thinking Jesus was a ghost. When Peter asked to walk out to meet Him, he was able to walk through the gushing waves and wind while he had his eyes on Jesus.

Then the wind took his attention away from Jesus and he was afraid and began to sink. *"Lord, save me!"* Peter said. Jesus wasted no time and immediately reached out His hand to catch him. *"You of little faith,"* Jesus said, *"why did you doubt?"*

It is so easy to become busy, distracted, and self-consumed. I find when this happens, I tend to worry more, I become more tired, stressed, and anxious about things that I am trying to keep within my control. And then I start feeling that tug at my heart. "Come to me," He says, "turn your eyes upon me and let me help you."

Jesus wants us to repeat His name over and over again – He delights in it. Our greatest obstacle is remembering to keep our eyes on Him, the One who saves us.

> For we have no power to face this vast army that is attacking us. We do not know what to do, but our eyes are on you.
> (2 Chronicles chapter 20 verse 12)

Chapter 27

PEACE ON EARTH

The stifling heat had escalated throughout the day and the humidity had given our skin a constant bathing. Tired, we all slept well that night until, early in the morning, we were awoken by an enormous crack of thunder that carried the power to shake the house, rattling the light fittings and shaking the display cabinet which was laden with china cups.

The rolling thunder and lightning carried on for some time as we lay awake in our beds waiting for it to pass.

The morning was filled with excited chatter about the previous night's storm. My youngest daughter looked puzzled, "What thunder?" She had slept peacefully throughout the storm.

Peace. Entering into the festive Christmas season, we sing songs about Peace On Earth though it can feel as though we are surrounded by chaos. Finding peace in times of chaos can seem very difficult. Finding peace in times of hardship and grief can seem impossible.

Each Christmas, we celebrate Jesus coming into this world as a baby. Beautiful images of the manger scene bring joy and love for the baby, the son of God, who came to save the world. It was the sacrifice this baby would grow up to make for us that brought the power to give us peace, peace that passes all understanding.

> But he was pierced for our transgressions, he was crushed for our iniquities; the punishment that brought us peace was on him, and by his wounds we are healed.
> (Isaiah chapter 53 verse 5)

The disciples were grief stricken when Jesus died. They did not recognise Him when He appeared to them on the road to Emmaus, and actually complained to Him that they had hoped that Jesus *"was the one who was going to redeem Israel,"* (Luke chapter 24 verse 21). Although they did not see it, He was standing in front of them fulfilling what the Scriptures had prophesied.

Jesus opened their eyes and when He appeared among them again, He said to them, *"Peace be with you,"* (Luke chapter 24 verse 36).

> Why are you troubled, and why do doubts rise in your minds? Look at my hands and my feet. It is I myself!
> (Luke chapter 24 verses 38-39)

The issue of peace

Sometimes it is easy to let problems take over our minds. Just like the disciples, we fret and are troubled over things we don't understand. Thanking God in everything reminds us that God is in control. Remembering that He is walking with us can replace our troubles with peace, and the peace in turn produces joy.

The peace that God gives us *"transcends all understanding"* (Philippians chapter 4 verse 7). Even when we go through the hardest of times and even if our circumstances do not change, God's peace can still be found when we remember He is present.

> "Though the mountains be shaken and the hills be removed, yet my unfailing love for you will not be shaken nor my covenant of peace be removed," says the Lord, who has compassion on you.
>
> (Isaiah chapter 54 verse 10)

As the disciples met with Jesus for the last time before He ascended into heaven, Jesus lifted up His hands and blessed them. It was while He was blessing them that He left them and was taken up into heaven, (Luke chapter 24 verses 51-2). Then they worshiped Him and returned to Jerusalem with great joy.

I can't help thinking that the blessing Jesus gave them was one of peace. Psalm chapter 29 verse 11 says:

> The Lord gives strength to his people; the Lord blesses his people with peace.

He knew that there would be hard times of persecution ahead for His disciples, but He left them with hearts full of joy and peace.

Each Christmas, as we give gifts to our loved ones, keep in mind the gift that God gives to you and allow yourself to be the receiver of peace.

> Peace I leave with you; my peace I give you. I do not give to you as the world gives. Do not let your hearts be troubled and do not be afraid.
> (John chapter 14 verse 27)

May you have peace in your hearts and an awareness of God's presence with you as you celebrate the gift of Jesus each Christmas.

Chapter 28

THANK YOU JESUS! A WORD FOR THOSE THAT WORRY

A few months ago, I attended a fundraiser. During one of the speeches, somebody on the other side of the room collapsed. The room fell silent, including the speaker. There was the sound of movement and a feeling of confusion from the end of the room where I was sitting as no one could see what had happened.

We waited, then heard a voice ask, "Is there a doctor in the room?"

My friend, who was sitting next to me, began to repeat the words, "Thank you Jesus," over and over again. It seemed strange to me at first, but as I pondered this, I was struck at what a very wise thing this was for her to do.

Saying these words took the fear out of the situation, put it back into the hands of The Creator and brought a sense of calmness and peace to an otherwise anxious moment. As the situation subsided and the person was treated by the doctor who was present, the room returned to order with many prayers I am sure, going up to heaven on her behalf.

My friend's words have resonated in my head ever since. Every time I find myself feeling anxious or stressed, I hear her words "thank you Jesus" even though it doesn't seem to make much sense.

When my car won't start or the bills are escalating, when I worry about providing for my family or can't see what the next few months are going to look like, why do the words "thank you Jesus" bring a calming effect? Why would I be saying thank you in a bad situation when it would be easier just to scream?

Generally, I forget. Feelings of worry tend to fall automatically when something goes wrong. Chords of anxiety tangle inside my stomach reaching up my neck to bring on a headache, but this is wrong. God didn't give us a spirit of fear and yet so often we let it have a hold.

The Bible tells us to bring all our thoughts captive (2 Corinthians chapter 10 verse 5). It says not to worry (Matthew chapter 6 verse 25). It also says to thank

God for everything (Ephesians chapter 5 verse 20). When things seem to be going wrong, the last thing we generally do feel is thankful, it just doesn't seem logical.

As I begin to practice saying thank you when it goes against everything I am feeling, (and can I just say, this is going to take me a long time to master) I begin to see the physical benefits of it.

I notice that my mind begins to clear, and the tangles of worry start to get torn down making a way for clearer thinking which often brings solutions that the worry wouldn't allow. I think my friend may be onto something.

By saying thank you when we least feel like it, we are actually saying to God:

- Thank you that You are bigger than this.
- Thank you for this opportunity to see Your hand at work.
- Thank you that whatever the outcome, You have a plan.
- Thank you that You have a purpose and nothing goes to waste.
- Thank you that through the pain, You are refining us.

- Thank you that nothing can separate us from the love of God.

Thank you God that You are in control.

Chapter 29

THE CHEERFUL GIVER

You can't have a perfect day without doing something for someone who'll never be able to repay you.
—John Wooden

I recently celebrated another birthday. Yes, I made the trip around the sun again and now I am another year older.

The night before my birthday, I was given strict instructions to stay in my room. I could hear my children busy in the kitchen and giggled to myself every time I saw my two youngest children peer through my bedroom door with loving smiles on their faces and, when spotted, they would come in to give me a hug for 'no apparent reason'.

Their excitement was inspiring and without knowing what they were up to, they had already given me the best gift without even knowing it – the gift of the cheerful giver.

There have been times when we have had to ask people to do things for us where we could offer no immediate reward or payment. The asking was difficult as feelings of being a burden on others and the fear of rejection came into play. But when people put their hands up of their own accord, God showed me something very beautiful.

In their giving, I saw the heart of God. Whether it was a sacrifice of prayer, money or time, the hearts of these cheerful givers filled my heart with gratitude and love for them, and taught me the value of a grateful giver like I have never seen it before. This in turn, has inspired me to want to be better at being a cheerful giver.

When people give with a smile on their face, it touches something deep inside that cannot be explained. When we give to others, we are not just giving them an object or something tangible, we are giving them an experience of the grace that comes from the heart of God.

I see clearly now why God loves a cheerful giver. It has nothing to do with the object, it is all about the measure of the heart.

When we give to the least of these, we give to God as we reflect His love within us. Next time you give, whether it be to God, a mission, a friend, or a complete stranger, keep in mind – there is so much more going on than you know.

> Give, and it will be given to you. A good measure, pressed down, shaken together, and running over, will be poured into your lap. For with the measure you use, it will be measured to you in return.
>
> (Luke chapter 6 verse 38)

Chapter 30

POEM— SHE DANCES

She dances in the morning sun,
    She twirls – her heart and body one.
    Her arms float skyward without bounds,
    And in her eyes her love is found.

    Of my gaze, she's unaware,
    The world around her is not bare.
    It's filled with flowers, butterflies,
    Only seen by angel eyes.

And in this world her heart takes flight,
    Up on her toes she does alight,
    To dance untethered, wild, and free,
    Just like a bird flies o'er the sea.

    Yet, in this beauty I behold,
    A little girl with heart so bold,
    And in the carousel of light,
    I see this little bird take flight.

Chapter 31

DOWNTON ABBEY AND A TRIP THROUGH ANOTHER AGE

> Teach them [God's words] to your children, talking about them when you sit at home and when you walk along the road, when you lie down and when you get up.
>
> Deuteronomy 11:19

Horse-drawn carriages, glamorous costumes, the grandeur of the old buildings, a slower pace of life, an era we never lived in – these are some of the things that I find intriguing about the BBC series Downton Abbey.

I loved getting to know the characters as they weaved through events that captured my imagination of a time gone by. It's so interesting to see a portrayal of a family set in a time of great leaps in innovation such as the invention of electricity, light bulbs, the telephone and the motor car which changed the world as they knew it, and then to see the devastation of the first world war and how it affected families and levelled the different classes of the day.

I look at the younger generations today and wonder if they ever consider what life was like before iPods, iPhones, Facebook, and texting. Do they think about a time when none of that existed? Or is it taken for granted that it must have always been there for they've never known life without it.

My mother-in-law has been arranging a recount of events that happened around her parent's wedding. Set in the year after World War Two, it was wonderful to read a real-life account of life back then.

Iris had to save a year's worth of rations to pay for the material needed to make her wedding dress, two bridesmaids gowns and two flower girl dresses but even then, there was not enough left over to make the long dreamed-of train for the wedding dress which had to be sacrificed.

The town they lived in was very cold at this time of the year and flowers had to be transported to Warwick from Brisbane. Unfortunately, communications broke down and the flowers never arrived. Transport was so expensive that the only family member on the groom's side to make it was Harry's dad but then he had to leave early to get home before the cold set in.

On Harry and Iris' honeymoon, they were the only passengers on a 14-hour freight train journey to Brisbane. They had to change trains at 3am and were exhausted when they finally arrived at their destination on Sunday morning. However, they still managed to make it to the 11am church service at the Salvation Army.

During the honeymoon week, Harry fell sick with what is believed to have been a relapse of Malaria from when he had it in the war. Iris nursed him back to health and Harry returned to work the following week.

It was certainly not a glamorous or easy start to their marriage nor was it the end of their trials, but their marriage of sixty-five years was a testament to how God brought them through very tough times together.

Some of our most precious possessions are photos and stories of days gone by. We tell them to our children so they can see where we've come from and how God has brought our family through adversity generation after generation.

In Deuteronomy chapter 4, God spoke to the Israelites before they entered the land that God had promised to them. He told them to remember what their children had not witnessed:

> Remember today that your children were not the ones who saw and experienced the discipline of The Lord your God: his majesty, his mighty hand, his outstretched arm ... (verse 2)

> It was not your children who saw what he did for you in the wilderness until you arrived at this place ... (verse 5)

> ... but it was your own eyes that saw all these great things The Lord has done.
> (verse 7)

Perhaps one of the greatest tools we can give our children to equip them in life are stories. Stories of how God brought us through our own wilderness, how He is a faithful God and although He disciplines us, He will bring us to our promised land whether here or in the life to come.

> ... be careful, and watch yourselves closely so that you do not forget the things your eyes have seen or let them fade from your heart as long as you live. Teach them to your children and to their children after them.
> (Deuteronomy chapter 4 verse 9)

Remember ...

Chapter 32

WORDS OF COMFORT FOR WHEN WE'VE BEEN TAKEN OUT OF OUR COMFORT ZONE

As we waited for the paramedics to arrive, my daughter clutched my shoulders as she struggled for breath. A very bad reaction to a migraine was having a spiralling effect on her. The instructions from the call centre were to keep her calm. I wanted to cry as I looked at her white frightened, clammy face, but I knew I had to muster every bit of strength in me to calm my distressed child.

Once on the scene, the paramedics managed to stabilise her breathing with calming words and a close eye on the heart monitor.

A calming effect
Words of comfort have much power. Power to heal, power to calm, power to change physical reactions, power to get our minds into a place of peace again.

Recently we moved house. As the men transported trailer loads and the women packed our house down for the fifth time in just over four years, my mother and mother-in-law spoke words of comfort to me: *"We will do whatever we can to help you,"* and *"We're happy to help, we love you. That's what family is for."*

Even though it was a job none of us wanted to do, these amazing women of God kept turning up with willing hearts, helping hands, a smile on their face and words of comfort. A new year, a house move, and beginning a new business all felt like entering unchartered territory.

Do you ever feel like God has taken you to the edge of what you think you can handle, and then beyond that? I can count on numerous occasions when that has happened. I think to myself, *God, this is just so hard! Can't we have some rest now?* and then, when I stop to listen to Him, the words of comfort come:

> With my strength, you can do this. I'm holding your hand. I am with you wherever you go. You will not do this alone.

Joshua's challenges

Joshua had some crazy challenges. In the very first verses of the book of Joshua, he was given a command:

> Moses my servant is dead. Now then, you and all these people, get ready to cross the Jordan River into the land I am about to give to them.
>
> (Joshua chapter 1 verse 2)

God then gives him a promise and confidence:

> I will give you every place where you set your foot, as I promised Moses ... No one will be able to stand against you all the days of your life. (verses 3-5)

And then the words of comfort came:

> As I was with Moses, so I will be with you; I will never leave you nor forsake you. Be strong and courageous, because you will lead these people to inherit the land I swore to their ancestors to give them. (verses 5-6)

And again:

> Be strong and courageous. Do not be afraid; do not be discouraged, for the Lord your God will be with you wherever you go.
>
> (verse 9)

Joshua was then able to go and give words of direction, confidence, and comfort to the people, and they listened.

> Whatever you have commanded us we will do, and wherever you send us we will go ... Only may the Lord your God be with you as he was with Moses ... be strong and courageous. (verses 16-18)

There was purpose in Joshua's challenges, there was a plan bigger than himself, there was a hope and there was help. God's firm direction and reassuring words gave Joshua the courage, belief, and confidence to go out and face his giants.

Bigger than the biggest giant
Joshua knew that his God was bigger than the physical giants that resided in the land. With his mind set on God, he was able to do the seemingly impossible and just as God had promised, He gave them every place they set their feet and God was with them everywhere they went.

I love this story. Our God is so much greater than the trials that try to shake us at the knees. Joshua's task was of exorbitant proportions; therefore, I know that my insignificant worries in the greater scheme of things, are well taken care of by a father who loves me, who knows my innermost thoughts just as He knew Joshua's.

He speaks directly to them, just as He spoke directly to Joshua. We just have to be quiet enough to hear it.

Chapter 33

THE LITTLE BOAT CALLED HOPE

After a very difficult and challenging year, we decided to have some time-out during the holidays by taking our little sailing boat on the river for some short runs.

My husband had spent a good part of the month restoring the little 'Mirror' sailboat. He'd carefully mended it, cleaned it and painted it. He skilfully crafted the artwork for the name, *Esperance* which means 'to hope' or 'in expectation'. It was ready to go, and we were very excited to take our little boat on its maiden voyage.

With grandparents in tow, we headed to the river. No sooner had we arrived when we realised that we had forgotten to bring the most important part. It was only a small piece, but without it our little boat would sail in circles with no direction. So, home we went to get the rudder.

Stepping into that little boat felt like the waves were washing away the cares of the world. The gentle lulling of the water lapping against the sides of the boat, the sound of the flapping of the sails, the sensation of the wind whispering past my ears and the warmth of the sun on my face made every weary thought vanish for a little while.

It was nice to sail on smooth seas for a time, but as we well know, there are many storms that life throws at us and life is not always smooth sailing.

Only two days later my husband and son took the Esperance out again, but this time into strong winds to see what it could handle. The sails whipped and the boat rocked threatening to topple. My husband took the boat into shelter where he and my son found refuge.

The previous year had been loaded with blessings as well as tragedy. In the February, Queen Elizabeth II celebrated her Diamond Jubilee, in June the world watched the last solar transit of Venus until 2117, and in July through to September we cheered during the Olympics and Paralympics held in London.

That same year also saw super storms, typhoons, massacres, and global financial downfalls, not to mention each person's individual triumphs and tribulations which are all part of the great roller coaster that we call life.

The hope of a new year

I love the hope that comes with a new year. We say goodbye to the old and somehow, with the difference of one night, the morning brings with it a new year, new opportunities, a resolution to eat better, live better and be better.

My Favourite Christmas carol, *Oh Holy Night* resonates with me all year long, especially the words, *'A thrill of light, the weary world rejoices for yonder lay a new and glorious morn.'*

Early in the new year, my town had already been belted with storms and mini tornadoes but in the midst of billowing clouds shines a light brighter than any other, a constant light that never goes out. His name is Jesus, the light of the world and He has the power to calm the rough seas in our lives.

> Therefore we will not fear, though the earth give way and the mountains fall into the heart of the sea, though it's waters roar and foam and the mountains quake with their surging.
> (Psalm chapter 46 verse 2)

With Jesus as our rudder pointing us towards the eternal light of God, we can rest in His everlasting arms for shelter. He is our refuge from the wind and the shelter from our storms.

There is a river whose streams make glad the city of God, The holy place where the Most High dwells. God is within her, she will not fall; God will help her at break of day. Nations are in uproar, kingdoms fall; He lifts his voice, the earth melts.

> (Psalm chapter 46 verses 4-6)

May the God of hope fill you with all joy and peace as you trust in him, so that you may overflow with hope by the power of the Holy Spirit.

> (Romans chapter 15 verse 13)

Chapter 34

CHRISTMAS, GATHERINGS AND ETERNAL TREASURES

We recently had a big family gathering for my husband's side of the family. We do this once a year, not so much as a 'Christmas' function but more so that we can meet up with family we wouldn't normally see. It is a great occasion, and I am always amazed at how much difference a year makes. Children of cousins who I once towered over, now look down at me from amazing heights!

"Where did that time go? When did you all grow up?" the adults said to the delight of the growing young teenagers. Then the kids ran off to play basketball and show each other the latest apps on their iPhones while we stood around talking about how old it makes us feel and how it doesn't seem that long ago that we were in their shoes (although at that age we had no idea what apps were, or iPhones for that matter!). How quickly life escapes us and how true the cliche, *make the most of every minute*!

A few years ago, a good friend of mine was diagnosed with cancer and later passed away from it. I remember our last conversation. She knew she didn't have long, and she was at peace about it. We talked about how one day we will meet on a beach in heaven somewhere and catch up on everything, and I have no doubt that one day we will, and she had no doubt either. I remember being astounded at the joy in her voice and thinking how amazing this precious girl was.

It was a bitter-sweet moment, and it was very difficult to finish that conversation, but I know where she is and that it is the place where she is most happy. You see, she had been storing up her treasures in heaven. Her love was for God, and she was so excited to be going to see Him.

Another impacting example of this was my husband's grandad. You would just have to mention the name 'Jesus' and his eyes would light up. He would tell us wonderful truths from the Bible, and he would glow like it was alive within him. He was so excited about the prospect of going to heaven that six months before he passed, he almost seemed disappointed when he survived an operation.

Although it has pained us greatly to lose loved ones in our lives, we are so grateful for the legacy they have left for us and the glimpse of heaven we saw in their eyes.

In the book of Matthew chapter 6 verses 19-21 Jesus says:

> Do not store up for yourselves treasures on earth, where moth and rust destroy, and where thieves break in and steal. But store up for yourselves treasures in heaven, where moth and rust do not destroy, and where thieves do not break in and steal. For where your treasure is, there your heart will be also.

One thing I want to see when I get to heaven is as many people that I know as possible. For, although I love Christmas and the wafting aroma of warm cinnamon in the baking gingerbread, the songs that evoke images of snow, log fires and sleighs being pulled by reindeers (even though in Australia we sit in sweltering heat), what I love most is the people who are a part of my life.

The smiles on wide-eyed children as they gaze at the Christmas lights on houses and manger scenes at the shopping centres. The coming together of communities to sing together at carol services. These are wonderful treasures and maybe minuscule glimpses of heaven on earth.

Chapter 35

LET YOUR LIGHT SHINE

My seven-year-old son recently brought me to tears. Although as toddlers, my children have brought me close to tears by using my brand-new lipstick to draw pictures on the mirror, or painting the walls with nappy cream or pouring litres of milk on my white carpet, this time was different. These were tears that came from an old lesson being brought to modern times through the kindness of a little boy. It was a simple act of kindness but one that carried enormous power.

A parent, from the school my children attend, approached my husband to tell him how touched he was by our son's actions. His son had forgotten his hat and had to sit out at lunchtime, missing out on playtime. My son gave him his own hat and let his friend go and play while he sat out and took his friend's punishment.

"That is amazing!" the parent said, "Who does that?"

This simple act reminded me of something Jesus would do. He was letting his light shine intuitively. This is not a story about my son but about the simple acts of kindness that surprise and bless because they are unusual in this day and age.

Have you ever noticed how 'crazed' people are at the supposedly 'happiest time of the year'? Shopping centres become a free-for-all, present-grabbing frenzy, leaving no room for manners, not to mention the car parking fiascos. If we survive pre-Christmas shopping uninjured, we definitely have something to praise the Lord for on Christmas Day!

But it is during this time that the smallest smile, the giving way, the 'after you', politeness in the smallest of forms, stands out as extremely memorable and heart-warming at the end of the day. The fact that someone has stopped to think of someone other than him or herself is, in effect, the very nature of God.

Philippians chapter two verses three and four says:

> Do nothing out of selfish ambition or vain conceit, but in humility consider others better than yourselves. Each of you should look not only to your own interests, but also to the interests of others.

History is rampant with the selfish desires of the human heart. It is by no means improving in today's world. We see its extreme effects in the suffering of abused and discarded children. We see it in the hoarding of wealth at the cost of the starving. We see it in the form of people dying alone, of the sick being unvisited, in schoolyard bullying, of drunken road-raging, and the list goes on. To think beyond oneself is not a difficult thing, it is only overlooked for the easier option of serving the self. Yet, to serve others brings joy that cannot be matched by selfish desires.

Consequently, a seven-year-old has reminded me once again that *"... the greatest of these is love"* (1 Corinthians chapter 13 verse 13) and how powerful that is!

Perhaps start with a smile and watch that spark catch fire, there's nothing quite so contagious. You never know who might just need it.

> You are the light of the world ... Let your light shine before men, that they may see your good deeds and praise your Father in heaven.
> (Matthew chapter 5 verses 14-16)

Chapter 36

HE LIFTED UP OUR CAR!

For Father's Day this year, my husband (along with most other fathers in our circle of friends) received a superhero movie, much to the excitement of our children.

Superheroes are big in our house, with costumes galore and heroic acts often being performed on our deck. It reminded me of a conversation between two of my children a few years ago:

Child no.1: "I wish superheroes were real".
Child no.2: "Dad's a real superhero – he lifted up our car!"

How did this come to be? Well apparently our four-year-old asked, "Dad, can you pick up a car?" So, he did, because in Tony's words, "I wanted to see if I could too!"

It still makes me laugh. Needless to say he was in a fair bit of pain for a few days after that, but the kids thought it was amazing! It became the topic of school show-and-tell presentations and conversations for months afterwards.

It doesn't quite need an act like lifting a car to be a superhero to children.

Mark Sholtez, a talented Australian singer/songwriter, wrote a song called *'Too Late for Heroes'*. He asks, *'Who's gonna save me? When it's too late for heroes and the world has gone crazy'*.

Our family met at the local tavern for Father's Day lunch this year. When we all get together it's hard to get a word in, but it is wonderful to observe the interactions and conversations. I especially enjoyed watching my son observe my dad and my father-in-law as they relayed their recent events and interactions along with fond memories of distant years across the table.

Although I couldn't hear everything from where I was sitting, I loved watching their expressions as there would be quiet, serious conversation over something perhaps tragic, then roars of laughter over some funny thing that had happened to one of them. What they may or may not realise is what a valuable teaching moment that was for my teenage son who was learning 'family values' in the subtle form of observation.

These men are my heroes

These men are my heroes. They have the wisdom of years, they have a love that has provided for and helped hold our families together for now three generations, and they have a strength and endurance that has come from the faith that they have in our Lord Jesus Christ.

My brother summed it up well recently on his Facebook post when he said:

> Today I am thankful for a good father who has raised me on a solid foundation. I am thankful that the solid foundation is the God of my father. I am also thankful to my Heavenly Father for so many blessings and for entrusting me to be a father too.

Having worked in child protection, my husband has seen the very tragic side of children growing up without fathers or with abusive, uninterested fathers. He has seen the pain of the children who have never known their fathers (and never will as there is no record of them), and how they are always looking for some family resemblance in people to see if – maybe that could be him? These children need a hero.

Micah chapter 6 verse 8 says:

> He has showed you, O man, what is good. And what does the Lord require of you. To act justly and to love mercy, and to walk humbly with your God.

Men and women alike can make positive changes to our nation through many ways, from their direct involvement in their own families as well as through other avenues. Our mission field is wherever and whatever we are doing – whether it's being a schoolteacher, an employee, a CEO, or a volunteer – our call to mission is everywhere.

However, for fathers particularly, their primary ministry is their family.

I am reminded of Malachi chapter 4 verse 6:

> He will turn the hearts of the fathers to their children, and the hearts of the children to their fathers; or else I will come and strike the land with a curse.

Dads, you are more powerful than you know. Use your powers for good and watch the world change.

Chapter 37

CATCH MY FALL

From where I sit, I can see the sky. As I look, there are two beautiful eagles circling way above every other bird. Strong, powerful creatures that fly as much with confidence as with elegance, and seem to own the air that they live in.

Our property is often nick-named 'Eagles Ridge' or 'Eagles Rest' by family, as it seems to be a favourite place for two of these amazing birds to catch the updraft.

As powerful as they are, once they reach 'lift off', they begin to soar, gliding as high as 2000m into the sky, where they rest on the winds that carry them without even so much as a beating of a wing for up to 90 minutes. (environment.nsw.gov.au)

Eagles have one partner in life and around mating season they perform amazing aerial acrobatics. One such display is when the eagle plummets at an incredible speed from a great height towards his mate, but quickly lifts just before he reaches her. She then turns onto her back in mid-air, and they lock talons (claws), flying in death-defying aerial loops together. (billabongsanctuary.com.au)

Leaning into the updraft
Challenges are a big part of life. My husband and I recently celebrated our 20th wedding anniversary. I am happy to say we are still very much in love.

On reflection, during the course of our marriage we have had times when we have soared to the heights of eagles with a seemingly clear view of what lay ahead of us, and we have had times when we have had to 'lock talons' so to say, and fly together on whirling rollercoasters of uncertainty and plummeting descents.

Thankfully, the up-draft has always caught us and we have been able to lean into it and glide, knowing that God is allowing us to rest on His strong and guiding winds when we know it is not in our power to do so.

The Bible's Old Testament tells us of some pretty big challenges the Israelites had to face. A major challenge for them was to trust God to take them out of Egypt where they had been slaves and oppressed for many years.

God Himself took up the fight and delivered His people away from their oppressors with many mighty miracles where the hand of God was unmistakable.

> You yourselves have seen what I did to Egypt, and how I carried you on eagle's wings and brought you to myself. Now if you obey me fully and keep my covenant, then out of all nations you will be my treasured possession. Although the whole earth is mine, you will be for me a kingdom of priests and a holy nation.
>
> (Exodus chapter 19 verses 4-6)

Soaring power
As God's children, we are His treasured possessions and He wants to carry us, He wants us to lean into His strength and let Him take up the battle on our behalf.

So often we try to do things in our own strength: we strive to fix problems; we toil to provide for our families; we want to be the fixer of relationships.

Toiling in our own strength will only make us weary.
In Isaiah chapter 40, God reminds us to fix our eyes back onto Him and remember who created the earth and who sits enthroned above the circle of the earth. He wants us to remember how powerful He is.

> "To whom will you compare me? Or who is my equal?" says the Holy One. Lift up your eyes and look to the heavens: Who created all these? He who brings out the starry host one by one and calls forth each of them by name. Because of his great power and mighty strength, not one of them is missing.
>
> (Isaiah chapter 40, verses 25–26)

He also wants us to know how tenderly He loves us too.

> He tends his flock like a shepherd: He gathers the lambs in his arms and carries them close to his heart; he gently leads those that have young.
>
> (Isaiah chapter 40, verse 11)

He knows that life makes us weary at times and has these words of hope for us:

> Even youths grow tired and weary, and young men stumble and fall; but those who hope in the Lord will renew their strength. They will soar on wings like eagles they will run and not grow weary, they will walk and not be faint.
>
> (Isaiah chapter 40 verses, 30–31)

Chapter 38

THE NIGHT OF THE LASAGNA DISASTER

Lasagne – it should be easy to make. It usually is, until you realise you are missing one simple ingredient – lasagne sheets. I was sure there was more in the cupboard, and it was too late to go to the shops.

The night of the lasagne disaster was a typical one in our household. Tony was studying while the children were doing homework and watching T.V. My eldest daughter was helping me cook, it was to be a great cooking lesson with Mum.

When the missing lasagne sheets discovery was made, there was no other choice. We had to do the best we could with the four small sheets that were left in the box, but it was no good. No matter which way we tried to arrange the mince and white sauce on the plate, it lacked solidarity. It was a splodge. A mess, with nothing to hold it up. A soupy splat on the plate. We just couldn't hide the fact that something was missing.

"Mum! What is this?" came the shocked cry of my food-critic teenage son.

Trying to stifle my giggles, I proudly replied, "This is lasagne son."

"No, it's not! It is not worthy of that name," he joked.

"Then, we shall call it white sauce and mince slop," I replied, to which we all broke out in laughter and then awkwardly ate the meal.

As I looked at this splat of formless lasagne on my plate, the old quote, *If you don't stand for something, you'll fall for anything* came to mind and we were able to turn the lasagne disaster into more than a cooking lesson, it became a life lesson.

What my lasagne was missing was some 'backbone' (metaphorically speaking of course).

You see, there are a lot of voices in the world vying for our attention. I guess the question is, do you know what you believe? Does your backbone keep you strong and sure-footed?

Ephesians chapter 4 verse 14 says:

> Then we will no longer be infants, tossed back and forth by the waves and blown here and there by every wind of teaching ...

Backbone

When I think of people with backbone, the Bible is full of heroes who stood for what they believed in even when it hurt. Take for instance: Shadrach, Meshach and Abednego who survived the fiery furnace; Daniel who survived the lion's den; Queen Esther who put her life on the line to save her people, and the list goes on.

Other heroes of the faith that come to mind are:

- William Wilberforce (1759-1833) – leader of the movement to abolish slavery.
- Abraham Lincoln (1809-1865) – campaigned against slavery.
- William Booth (1829-1912) – founder of the Salvation Army with a heart for suffering humanity.
- Eglantyne Jebb (1876 - 1928) – founder of the 'Save the Children' foundation.
- Mother Teresa (1910-1997) – cared for the sick and poor of Calcutta, and
- Nelson Mandela (1918-2013) – anti-apartheid activist and served as the first president of South Africa.

Modern day men and women with backbones still exist and as a result, they make a difference in the world today in the hope that the world tomorrow will be a better place to live in.

People who see a need and who can't take one more step without doing something to make somebody else's life better, even though it may cost them something, are more valuable than they are given credit for. While we still have millions of children being trafficked and people starving across the world, there is room for more heroes.

> *I've learned that courage was not the absence of fear, but the triumph over it. The brave man is not he who does not feel afraid, but he who conquers that fear.*
> -Nelson Mandela

Do you relate to that feeling that nags at your heart and pains you to do something to help someone? To say something, to speak up when others are being shouted down? Be it seemingly small or on a big scale, all acts of kindness are significant, especially to those who benefit from them.

So, I encourage you ...

> Be strong and courageous. Do not be afraid; do not be discouraged, for the Lord your God will be with you wherever you go.
> (Joshua chapter 1 verse 9)

Chapter 39

HAVE I LOVED YOU ENOUGH TODAY?

Raindrops on roses – this is what awaited me one morning when I peered through the window at my potted rose plant which had recently bloomed the most delicious smelling, deep pink bud I had ever seen it grow.

Each time I glanced its way, it had grown a little bigger and leaned in as if beckoning me to step out onto the deck, hold its beautiful head in my hands and breathe in its perfume.

This rose brought so much joy to my week and made me pause numerous times throughout my busy days. It slowed me down and caused me to literally stop and smell the roses.

After a few days of watching the rose grow from a promise to a bud, to a bloom, it lifted its head as if it so dearly wanted to be admired. It was breathtaking. I took every spare moment to enjoy it, taking photos and posting them to social media. It couldn't have bloomed any brighter than it did on that day even if it tried, and somehow, I knew I had to make the most of it.

Overnight, a warm wind picked up and the very next day, the rose was gone. I must admit, I felt sad. This rose that had brought me so much joy was now a flutter of petals, scattered across the grass.

I was glad I had enjoyed the rose while it was there. I was glad I had taken the time to appreciate its beauty.

Moments are fleeting. Through all the busyness, distractions and demands, my children and loved ones are like that rose. They make me want to slow down, to hold their faces in my hands and kiss their cheeks. They make me want to take mental photographs of moments that will imprint in my heart forever.

They make me want to hold their hands and tell them time and time again that I love them – which I do. And though it may seem a little over the top, I don't want a single day to go by that they do not know how much they are loved.

We live in uncertain times. Each day is a gift. Yet in amongst the busyness, in amongst the demands, in amongst the battles, there are roses in the form of loved ones whose faces want to be seen, whose eyes long to be looked into, whose hands want to be held.

YOU COULD BE DANCING

If today is our last day on this earth, have we loved enough? Have we enjoyed the faces that are before us? Our spouses, our children, our parents, our friends? Have we forgiven and let go of offences that tangle and eat away at the love that could have been shared. When perspective takes hold, have we loved as we've been loved?

Before the petals fly into the wind, take opportunities as they present themselves to make eye contact, smile deeply, love deeply and breathe in every moment. There are only so many moments in life.

> The grass withers and the flowers fall, but
> the word of our God endures forever.
> (Isaiah chapter 40 verse 8)

In the words of singer/songwriter Sara Groves:

> *'And at the risk of wearing out my welcome.*
> *At the risk of self-discovery,*
> *I'll take every moment,*
> *And every minute that you give me.*
> *And I wish all the people I love the most*
> *Could gather in one place,*
> *And know each other and love each other well.*
> *And I wish we could all go camping.*
> *And lay beneath the stars,*
> *And have nothing to do and stories to tell.*

*We'd sit around the campfire
And we'd make each other laugh,
Remembering when ...
And you're the first one I'm inviting.
Always know that you're invited, my friend.*

*And at the risk of wearing out my welcome.
At the risk of self-discovery,
I'll take every moment,
And every minute that you give me.*

(Sara Groves, 'Every minute')

Chapter 40

POEM - IT'S YOU
(by Tony R. Moore)

You are the light of my day, the peace of my night;
the joy that inspires a life lived with others in mind.

You grace time like the embrace of a gentle breeze
as it fills the sail of a still boat in calm waters on a summer's day.

You lead by serving, speak by listening and empower by loving.
You cheer from the heart, heal from the hand and embrace just by living.

It is you, the most impressive of women,
whom my heart wills to shadow.

It is you that rain falls on more sweetly,
that a slow fire warms more sincerely.

In a field of a million flowers there is none that stand so tall;
smell so pleasing and radiate so freely as you
who are busy lifting others up so they can see.

You are my favourite place to be,
It is you that I love, and you that love me.
Forever & Always.

Happy 40th birthday – forever and always – love me xoxo

ABOUT THE AUTHOR

Rebecca lives on the Sunshine Coast, Australia
with her husband and four children.

On a rainy day you will find Rebecca wrapped up in a
blanket, huddled around a fireplace with a good book, a
piano, a cup of hot chocolate or two and her five most
favourite people distracting her from her work.

An internationally published writer and author, her passion is
to inspire others through:

WORDS
that capture and present the beauty in life

LOVE
the simplicity of everyday moments and

HOME
to provide value to being a woman,
wife, mother, daughter and friend to all.

Rebecca's professional goal is to
write words that bring life, hope and healing, drawing people
closer to the light of God, the hope of this world.

His name is Jesus and He is our home.

Pizza & Choir

A walk through the garden of life that leads you home.

By Rebecca Moore

ALSO BY REBECCA MOORE:

PIZZA & CHOIR

With a masterful touch, loving heart,
and joyful perspective on life, Rebecca captures and retells
the moments in our lives that really matter.

The second in the series of
SHORT REAL-WORLD DEVOTIONALS THAT MAKE YOU FEEL NORMAL,
this collection of short stories, poems and prose
will brighten your everyday,
have you smiling, laughing out loud, crying,
and making the most of life's precious moments.

ISBN: 978-0-6484602-0-6

SHORT REAL-WORLD DEVOTIONALS THAT MAKE YOU FEEL NORMAL

"The sound of heaven can be heard clearly...bringing light, life and love from heaven above."
—Pastor Steve Penny

Where Rivers Flow

Finding your way out of the desert with joy and gladness

REBECCA MOORE

WHERE RIVERS FLOW

Take a moment to sail down the river with Rebecca as she talks life, love and the promises of God.

The third in the series of SHORT REAL-WORLD DEVOTIONALS THAT MAKE YOU FEEL NORMAL, *Where Rivers Flow* continues the easy conversation and beautiful poetry that you fell in love with in her first two books *You Could Be Dancing* and *Pizza & Choir*.

Where Rivers Flow takes you deep into the love of Jesus. You'll find yourself again laughing and reflecting at everyday situations that draw us closer to God and the beauty of home, while drinking in the warmth of her timeless poetry that takes you into another realm.

This is the refreshing drink you've been looking for.

ISBN: 978-0-6453697-6-2

You can find Rebecca online at:
- www.rebeccamoore.life
- instagram.com/rebeccamoore_author
- facebook.com/Rebecca Moore – Author

www.ingramcontent.com/pod-product-compliance
Lightning Source LLC
Chambersburg PA
CBHW032038290426
44110CB00012B/851